Care & Cooking of
Fish & Game

Care &
Cooking of
Fish
&
Game

JOHN WEISS

Winchester Press
Tulsa, Oklahoma

Library of Congress Cataloging in Publication Data

Weiss, John, 1944–
    Care & Cooking of Fish & Game.

        Includes index.
        1. Cookery (Game). 2. Cookery (Fish). 3. Game and
game-birds, Dressing of. 4. Fishes, Dressing of.
I. Title.
TX749.W37   641.6'91   81-16302
ISBN 0-87691-358-3   AACR2

Published by Winchester Press
1421 South Sheridan Road
P.O. Box 1260
Tulsa, Oklahoma 74101

Book design by Quentin Fiore

Printed in the United States of America

1 2 3 4 5   86 85 84 83 82

For Jeff and Tom, budding outdoorsmen

Acknowledgments

My sincere appreciation goes out to the editors of The American Hunter, Fur-Fish-Game, Petersen's Hunting, *and* Sports Afield *for allowing me to revise, update and reprint portions of various chapters which originally appeared in those publications.*

Contents

Preface

In addition to the recreational benefits of hunting and fishing, out-doorsmen find themselves rewarded with a special bonus that neither golfers, tennis players, football fans nor followers or participants of any other sport are able to enjoy. They acquire delicious food they can take home for the dinner table. And in these days of spiraling inflation and periodic shortages of almost everything, that is a welcome way of paring the family grocery bill. Even more than that, the monetary value of a home freezer filled with fish and game helps to compensate for part of the equipment and travel expenses associated with rod and gun pursuits.

Anyone who is just as concerned with good health as good eating should appreciate still other rewards of the hunter's gamebag or fisherman's creel. You simply cannot buy meat that is as fresh, flavorful and nutritious as that which is harvested yourself. Compared to domestic livestock, most fish and game meats are quite low in cholesterol. Also, they are not pumped full of artificial flavors and coloring agents, water (which makes ham and some other domestic meats weigh more so you have to pay more), preservatives, and a whole raft of chemical additives that may produce harmful long-term effects.

It is an unfortunate state of affairs these days that sportsmen, along with politicians and oil company executives, are often victims of unjustified character assassination. Behind a number of rods and rifles are well-meaning but inexperienced sportsmen who give a bad name or image to their sport.

Such outdoorsmen may be able to wield fly rods or shotguns like experts, yet in many instances they are largely lacking in other skills related to their sports, such as filleting fish, field-dressing deer or plucking geese. Or perhaps there is some other void in their education, such as not knowing the proper way to transport fish long distances without spoiling, how to cut up a big-game animal into prime steaks and roasts, how to freeze fish and game, or which cooking methods are best for specific species.

All of these are key elements in successfully achieving the most desirable end result, which is a table surrounded with smiling faces asking for second helpings. If this book helps make that a regular occurrence in your home, its goal will have been achieved.

JOHN WEISS
Chesterhill, Ohio

1

Caring for Your Catch

Few outdoor ramblings offer greater satisfaction than using fishing knowledge and skill to find your quarry and then entice it to strike. Those anglers who boat a trophy gamefish, photograph it quickly and then slip it back into the water to fight again another day receive my highest respect and admiration. They, indeed, have reached the pinnacle of sportsmanship. But in addition to catching and releasing fish, any angler worth his salt occasionally enjoys eating them, too.

For any who may be inclined to question the killing of fish as out of line with sound conservation practices, we should take a minute here to emphasize that, unlike oil and many other limited resources, virtually all fish species are renewable. Admittedly, there are a few exceptions in which the very specific habitat required by certain fish is incessantly destroyed by the bulldozers of modern times. But largely, through the continued support of the management programs implemented by our fish and game agencies, we can expect to enjoy abundant fish populations and reasonable – in some cases, even liberal – harvest quotas almost indefinitely.

In many instances fishery biologists even recommend that certain species *not* be released under any conditions. One example that readily comes to mind is panfish such as bluegills, sunfishes, perch and crappies. These feisty little brawlers are so prolific that it's common for them to rapidly exceed their available food supply. When this occurs, individuals become stunted. The best thing that can happen to them is having their numbers regularly thinned.

Many inland lakes and reservoirs develop thermoclines in summer and consequently are stocked with trout of various species that may occupy a cold-water niche which the customary warm-water fish in the body of water do not use. For all practical purposes these particular hatchery-raised trout are sterile. Fishery managers refer to this state of affairs as "put and take" fishing because they have planted the trout not necessarily to benefit the ecosystem, but merely for anglers to enjoy.

However, the trout just described should not be confused with native strains found in northeastern streams, rivers of the upper Midwest, streams and dam tailwaters coursing through the Appalachian and Ozark Mountain ranges, western rivers in the higher elevations, alpine lakes throughout the Rocky Mountain states, or any other place where trout naturally reproduce and are valuable (though nevertheless renewable) assets of their habitat.

Nor should the sterile lake fish described above be confused with the impressive salmonid fishery that exists in the Great Lakes, where rainbow trout, brown trout, steelhead, lake trout, coho salmon and chinook (king) salmon either make successful spawning runs up feeder tributaries or prepare redds on shallow shoreline shoals.

Great Lakes trout and salmon are unique in that the question of whether to release them is not always cut and dried. When the fish are in shallow water with intentions of spawning, and have slowly acclimated themselves to the warmer water temperatures, they usually will survive to complete their courtship if handled carefully and released. During the summer months, however, when the fish are in the main-lake areas seeking out 50-degree water, which often exists at depths of 60 to 100 feet, the fish are not likely to survive release when wrenched from such depths. Trout and salmon typically experience the "bends," plus the added shock of suddenly much warmer surface waters. They simply cannot tolerate such trauma.

The striped bass stocked in inland bodies of sweet-water is another species that should not be released unless specific regulations or size limits require anglers to do so. Stripers, too, are highly vulnerable to stress and when fought on hook and line produce excessive amounts of lactic acid in their muscles, a condition which commonly causes the fish to perish shortly after release.

The point in all of this is that while in many cases applause should be given the sportsman who regularly releases many of his fish, there are many situations in which keeping the catch for the table is not only ethically permissible but strongly recommended.

Another thing crucial to our discussion is that no matter which particular recipe may be decided upon, the quality of fish cannot be improved by any cooking method if it is mishandled to begin with. For this reason, properly caring for one's catch becomes of paramount concern the very moment a fish is landed.

Onboard Fish-Storage Methods

Nationwide, one of the most common methods of storing fish during a day on the water is the use of some type of stringer. At last count I owned about five such stringers. Several are of the metal chain-link design with squeeze-type snaps. Another, which looks very much the same, consists of a nylon cord and sliding hard-nylon snaps, each of which has a special locking feature. I also have a couple of cord-type stringers lying around. These are the kind with a brass ring at one end of a nylon rope and a pointed skewer at the other.

Any fisherman probably owns a stringer of at least one or perhaps all of these types. But I have a confession to make: except during rare circumstances, which I'll describe later, I almost never use any of these stringers for actually keeping fish. They are simply tucked away somewhere and occasionally used for brief minutes at the end of the day when I want to secure several fish on the snaps in order to take a picture.

The use of stringers often is responsible for the rapid deterioration of freshness and flavor in fish. Use them only in cool, clean water.

The primary reason I seldom use stringers is because I'm purely infatuated with fresh-fish dinners and therefore always strive to ensure that all the flavor I catch ultimately ends up on the dinner table.

There are numerous ways in which flavor and freshness can be lost, because any fish you catch must pass through many stages of handling. After they are landed, they must be stored in some manner throughout the remainder of the day's fishing. Then they must be transported to your home, cleaned, perhaps frozen to be defrosted weeks later and, finally, cooked by the method of your choice. If any one of these steps is bungled, the resulting fish dinner is likely to be uneventful, at best.

We've all had the experience of a bad fish dinner. With some people the memories linger so long they never give fish a second chance, and I'm willing to go on record as stating that the use of stringers often does more to harm the flavor of fish than anything else. Picture the following scenario which I have witnessed on countless occasions: Joe Angler is fishing when suddenly his arm is jolted by the strike of a hard-fighting bass or perhaps a lunker walleye. Joe does a commendable job of playing and eventually landing his prize. Since it has come from 15 feet deep where the water is cool, the fish's flesh is firm and displays vibrant colors. But from that point on, the fisherman does almost nothing right. The trophy is admiringly clipped onto a chain stringer and slipped over the side of the boat where the fish drags as Joe continues his efforts for another six hours.

The surface waters of almost any lake, reservoir or sluggish river, especially during the popular fishing months, are usually algae-saturated and sometimes laced with traces of gasoline and oil. The temperature of these surface waters under a blazing summer sun may often approximate air temperatures. During the months of June through September it is not at all unusual for the surface to register 60, 70 or even 80 degrees! In the deep South, in shallow impoundments water temperatures sometimes reach 90 degrees! If the day's fishing is during a rainy period the water may be roiled with mud, silt, decomposed bottom debris and who knows what else.

It isn't long before Joe's fish turns belly-up, rigor mortis sets in and the wild, distinctive hues it once displayed fade to mottled gray or dull white.

Sound preposterous? The truth of the matter is that this is exactly the treatment too many fishermen give their catch.

Most live wells in boats are just efficient means of gassing and polluting your catch, because the fish are stored in warm, dirty surface water. One way to make a live well more effective is by converting it into a totally self-enclosed system.

But that is not the end of the story. After a long day's fishing a substantial number of anglers, tired and weary, simply throw their catch onto a pile of newspapers in a hot car trunk and let their fish "slow cook" during the drive home. Joe's fish may then lie on the back porch for still another hour while he has dinner. Dressing and freezing the catch may not come until the wee hours of the night.

Will Joe's catch result in a gourmet meal that members of his family will file with their fond memories? Hardly. No matter how the fish is prepared, predictably they'll walk away from the table with curled lips and silent vows never to eat fish again. It is a very sad state indeed.

A live well or holding tank in your boat doesn't help matters much, despite the fact that they are used in catch-and-release bass fishing tournaments. Undoubtedly, an aerated live well does a better job than a stringer of keeping fish alive that are later to be weighed and then set free, because they are not stressed to the degree they would be if they were dragged around all day by metal snaps through their jaws. A live well also eliminates the troublesome bother of having to string each individual fish and repeatedly lift the stringer into the boat with every change of fishing location. But all live wells store fish you intend to eat in the same warm, crummy surface water that a stringer might otherwise hang in. All you've really achieved is a more efficient method of gassing and polluting your catch.

The bottom line is that fish destined for the dinner table will be far more flavorful if given entirely different treatment. One way to use a live well for onboard storage of fish you plan to eat is to make the well a fully enclosed, self-contained system that is free of warm, dirty or polluted surface water. First put in the live well's drain plug, then fill it with unchlorinated tap, well or spring water, add a cake of ice to ensure the water remains cool and finally turn on the aerator for a few minutes now and then (never let an aerator run continuously as the fish will die of oxygen poisoning).

An even more practical method of storing fish onboard is through the use of a conventional camping cooler filled with ice. Anglers often employ such a cooler anyway for sandwiches and drinks, and those models with a 30-quart capacity or larger are ideal.

I own and religiously use several such coolers, each with a different capacity depending upon the size of the boat I plan to work out of on any given day. The largest unit, and my favorite, is a jumbo 80-quart cooler made by Coleman, which I use in my 18-foot bass boat and find perfectly suited to storing food and drinks for three fishermen during the day, in addition to any fish we may retain.

When fishing from smaller craft, such as my 14-foot aluminum V-bottom or 12-foot johnboat, I use a 40-quart Thermos cooler or a 30-quart model made by Igloo. Other quality coolers are made by Cronco, Norcold and Sears, to name a few. Whatever the brand, when considering a cooler primarily to be used for the storage of fish there are a number of features to look for.

I like a cooler with a sturdy lid that can also serve as a seat if space onboard is at a premium. The lid also should be tight-fitting to ensure maximum retention of cold. The hinges and latch assembly should be of heavy-duty, non-rust materials; there should be some type of draincock near the bottom of the cooler for releasing melted ice water. Lastly, be sure your chosen cooler has sturdy carrying handles, because when it's loaded with ice, food, drinks and fish the total weight of the unit can climb rapidly.

Regardless of the style of cooler you select, cracked or crushed ice will do a much better job of preserving fish than a single large block (cubes work fine, too, or you can break a large block into numerous chunks with an ice pick), simply because hundreds of individual pieces of ice afford more total cold surface area than a single block. I usually fill my cooler with ice at home the night before I plan to fish in order to save time the following morning and also to pre-condition the inside of the chest so it is as cold as possible. The internal temperature of any quality cooler can be maintained at about 38 degrees by an ample quantity of ice for about 20 hours in moderately warm weather without a need to replenish the supply.

On top of the ice place several plastic bags (I prefer Ziploc poly bags, available at any grocery store, but others that can be closed with twist-ties are fine) and slip your fillet knife and whetstone into your tackle box.

Each time a fish which you desire to keep for the table is boated, immediately give it a sharp rap over the head just behind the eyes to kill it. At this time, some anglers like to slit open the belly of the fish and remove the innards. If you simply drop the entrails overboard they will sink to the bottom and quickly be devoured by catfish, crayfish, turtles and other scavengers. However, the most important thing is that the fish be placed in a plastic bag, the opening closed and the package completely buried in the crushed ice, quickly. With this technique there is no muss, no fuss and no messy ice chest to clean later. And re-

The ideal way to store fish onboard is in a plastic bag submerged in ice in a camping cooler. Even on the hottest days your catch will remain icy cold and fresh.

gardless of the temperature that day, your fish will remain icy cold and fresh. Too much trouble? The procedure just outlined should take less than one minute per fish, a small price to pay for the guarantee that you'll be preserving all the flavor you've caught.

We're speaking here of bass, walleyes, panfish, trout or any other fishes that are not likely to weigh more than four or five pounds apiece or measure more than 20 inches or so in length. If you're going after the big ones, such as northern pike or lake trout, the ideal method of storage is exactly the same; you'll simply have to plan in advance to have a larger cooler and larger plastic bags.

When you dock your boat at the end of the day, before heading

The best solution to the problem of storing very large fish is a jumbo fish box. Using plywood, you can build a model that will last years for less than $25.

home, finish dressing or filleting the fish (instructions are given in Chapter 2). To make this chore easy, I have bolted a piece of exterior-grade plywood to the lids of each of my coolers. The rough side of the plywood up provides a handy non-slip cutting surface for dressing fish. And with the work done shoreside you won't infuriate other members of the family by dripping and splattering the kitchen with messy fish cleanings. In an increasing number of regions, marinas and fishing camps have special fish-dressing facilities available for public use. Otherwise, use your cutting board and a pail of clean water. The scraps and cleanings can be placed in one plastic bag for easy, clean deposit in the nearest trash can and the fillets or dressed fish can be placed in another bag and secured in the ice again for the trip home.

If you are fishing from a bass boat or any other craft with a built-in live well, and equipment space is minimal, one alternative to using a camping cooler is to screw in the well's drain plug and then fill the live box itself with ice to take the place of a cooler. Since live wells are not insulated the ice won't last as long, but the fish nevertheless receive far better treatment than if continually dragged through warm surface waters on a stringer. The fish can remain in the live well for the entire trip home, but remember to use the plastic bags. Fish allowed to soak and slosh around in the melt water in the bottom of a live well or cooler will be blah and tasteless.

Still another option is available to those who either own large center-console boats or other offshore rigs, or who frequently hire a charter craft in order to fish any of the Great Lakes for trout or salmon that may weigh as much as 35 pounds or more. In situations like this, even the largest coolers generally are too small, so many enterprising anglers merely make their own. All it takes is a $25 investment and a Saturday afternoon.

Such a cooler can be fabricated from ½-inch-thick plywood. Make the box rectangular and approximately three feet long by two feet wide by two feet high. Bolt on heavy-duty hinges, handles and other hardware. From any automotive supply store, buy a small, inexpensive kit containing fiberglass cloth and resin to finish the inside of the box so it will be completely sealed and watertight. Some anglers even go to added lengths by making insulated liners of inch-thick sheet styrofoam, but the simple model described above will perform adequately over a period of many years whenever you need to ice down overly large fish.

If you're faced with a long drive home at the end of the day, and may be on the road several hours, leave your cooler sitting in your boat as it rides on its trailer, or set the cooler on the back seat of your car with a nearby window open. In both cases the idea is to allow breezes and fresh air to continually circulate around the ice chest. Never stow a cooler in your locked car trunk where midsummer temperatures may reach 120 degrees.

Sometimes, however, it may not be practical to tote a full-size cooler on a fishing outing. Such is often the case when angling from a small canoe, johnboat or inflatable raft. In these situations I sometimes make use of two burlap bags, which can usually be obtained free at any feed or farm supply store.

The fish are killed and placed in their plastic bags as usual, but then slipped between the layers of burlap which have been thoroughly soaked with water. Evaporation and slight breezes, even on the warmest days, will keep your catch cool and fresh in this manner. If at all possible, try to ensure that the burlap is placed in the shade underneath a boat seat or in some other location where it will not be exposed to the direct rays of the sun.

Shoreside Fish Storage

A vast number of this country's anglers do not use boats, preferring instead to either wade or work the shorelines and beaches. Some may be dry-fly anglers probing famed Adirondack waters in upstate New York; others may be surfcasters working the Atlantic coast. The pleasure another angler seeks may be tossing tiny spinners to bass and panfish in an Indiana farm pond, while yet another's delight may be backpacking into remote lake areas in Montana's high country where golden trout have never seen an angler's lure.

Whatever the setting, there can be an iced-down cooler waiting back in the car, dune buggy or four-wheel drive vehicle. But the common denominator is that all of these anglers seek their quarry while traveling by shank's mare so it probably isn't practical to have a cooler immediately near where one is fishing. Consequently, other stopgap remedies must be sought if the fresh flavor of the catch of the day is to be preserved.

For generations, trout anglers have traditionally made use of wicker or canvas creels, but they work just as well for panfish, small bass and similar species. When using such a creel it is not necessary to secure individual fish in plastic bags as no ice is involved, and hence, there is no accumulation of melt water. My preference is to partially fill the creel with fresh green ferns or moss that first have been soaked with water and then only slightly wrung out. Place the fish in the creel on top of the vegetation, then cover the catch with additional damp ferns or moss.

The fabric of canvas creels and the construction of wicker creels is porous to allow the circulation of air, which results in a cooling effect through evaporation of the moisture in the vegetation. In scorching hot weather the outside surfaces of canvas and wicker creels can also be periodically soaked with water to further aid in cooling the fish inside.

If only brief stretches of water are being fished before returning to a vehicle and driving on, the old burlap bag trick can again come into play. Soak the burlap as usual and place it under the shade of a nearby tree.

Keep in mind that burlap bags, canvas creels and wicker creels are only intended to serve as temporary fish-storage methods. They are good for possibly three or four hours at most, and you should make plans to transfer your fish to a much colder storage area as soon as convenience allows.

If the water is clean and cold, or at least cool, and the weather likewise, stringers of assorted sizes and designs may now, and only now, come into justifiable use. I'm thinking mainly of those clean, frigid waters in northern Canada where pike, walleyes and brook trout reign supreme, or in sub-arctic waters where grayling, char and lake trout are the sought-after species. Yet it's also possible to use stringers in more southerly latitudes, for example, during the famed spring walleye runs or opening days in Minnesota, Wisconsin, Michigan and Ohio, the exciting shad runs that see anglers flock to Maryland and Delaware, or the late fall and midwinter steelhead and salmon runs in Michigan and Wisconsin.

Whatever the location, there are specific dos and don'ts regarding the use of stringers, and these apply to boat anglers as well as those who don hip boots or chest waders.

When securing a fish on a stringer, the intention is to keep the fish alive, so don't run the cord or metal snap through the fish's gill-cover opening and out the mouth as this will kill it in short order. Also, never run a stringer through both the upper and lower lips as this prevents a fish from opening and closing its mouth, which is necessary for it to pump its gill covers and therefore breathe.

Simply run the stringer once through the thin skin just beneath and behind the lower jaw and the fish will be sufficiently secured. Crowding too many fish on a short stringer will serve no useful purpose, and dragging fish on a stringer in the wake of an outboard will drown them.

Still another alternative that finds favor among anglers who are either hoofing it to their fishing haven or using a lightweight cartop boat is making use of an insulated picnic bag that can be set in the shade of a shoreline tree or slipped underneath a boat seat. Buy a bag designed to hold two thermos bottles, with a lid-type flap that can be tightly closed with a zipper or several Velcro fasteners.

Using ice with one of these picnic bags is somewhat difficult and often messy. I prefer one of those thin, rectangular, reusable ice packs you can buy in any camping supply store. These gizmos are filled with liquid refrigerant, completely sealed, and intended to be placed in your home freezer until they are frozen solid. You can then transfer such an ice pack to your picnic bag and it will efficiently cool everything inside for about 12 hours. When you arrive home, merely return the ice pack to your freezer so it will be ready the next time you decide to go fishing.

Finally, several random thoughts come to mind, off-beat methods of fish preservation that do a creditable job of keeping fish cold when other equipment is not available.

I'm reminded, for example, of an elk hunt in Wyoming's high country several years ago. It was customary to pursue those great beasts during the very early morning hours and then again as twilight came. During the midday hours we fished small streams and alpine lakes for cutthroat trout. The guides and outfitters, who usually joined us in the fun, for convenience simply stuck their fish into handy snowbanks, their tails poking out to mark their locations. Maybe it was the wilderness atmosphere of it all, or it might have been the near-freezing storage method – I suspect both – but those trout were without question the best I've ever tasted.

No, I take that back. During a number of ice-fishing adventures for trout, and also panfish, we later speared off dinner platters with as much enthusiasm. When ice fishing, of course, we merely leave

When you're ice fishing, nature cooperates by providing instant refrigeration. Just toss your fish on the ice until you're ready to go home.

the catch where it falls and it is perfectly preserved for any length of time. Again, it's that magic coldness that locks in flavor and freshness.

Another time we were surfcasting for bluefish and striped bass off the Atlantic shore at Sandy Hook, New Jersey. There, and elsewhere along the eastern seaboard, clambakes and midnight fishfries on moon-drenched beaches are what keep men from growing old. One popular way of preserving freshly caught fish is by laying a bed of sopping wet seaweed on the sand, then the fish, more seaweed on top, then covering the works with a tarp that is regularly sloshed down with water. I've heard that in southern California, yellowtail anglers use a similar ruse with beds of kelp.

I've also seen surfcasters dig down two feet through the warm, dry, white sand and into the underlying layer that is brown, damp and cool. Fish buried in these deep, dark repositories do nearly as well as if they were in a refrigerator, but you had better mark their locations with driftwood or flags or it may take hours of rooting around later to find your supper!

Transporting Fish Long Distances

Common ice chips or cubes in a camping cooler will do an acceptable job of temporarily keeping fish well-chilled during a day or two of driving, but in hot weather the ice may have to be replenished as often as every 12 or 15 hours.

But what about transporting fish great distances, as during vacation trips or when you embark upon that special, once-a-year, far-away adventure. The return leg may see you on the road for several days or more, which really is too long to keep fish "on ice." With fish, flavor loss is directly proportional to the length of time that natural bacterial action is allowed to work on the muscle fibers.

After about the third day, it is essential that any further bacterial action be immediately halted. The only way to accomplish this is by radically changing the environment in which bacteria can otherwise speedily grow and continue to break down tissue. In other words, the fish must be frozen, as bacteria may continue to live in that state of preservation but are incapable of rendering further damage because of their inactive or dormant condition.

Let's say you're an angler who lives in Oklahoma and you'll be driving to a lake in Ontario for pike and walleye fishing. Like most fishermen, during the initial days of your stay at a fishing resort or while tent camping, you'll probably eat some of what you catch and release the others. During the last couple of days you'll likely begin accumulating a legal quantity of fish to take back home to your family. This means that almost immediately after hitting the road for home, you should freeze your fish. But how?

Dry ice is the secret!

I usually stop in the first major city I come to and check a phone book's Yellow Pages for the location of the nearest dairy, ice cream factory, or meat-packing plant. These are the most common sources of dry ice, but if you look under the "refrigeration" section others may also be listed. I drive to the nearest facility and obtain a quantity of dry ice to replace the crushed ice that was temporarily used in my camping cooler.

Dry ice is carbon dioxide (CO_2) which has been frozen to minus-109 degrees Fahrenheit, a temperature at which it remains as it gradually dissipates over a period of time. Chemists call the breakdown of dry ice "sublimation" — the direct transformation from a solid state to a gaseous state with no resulting formation of liquid. Dry ice freezes meat five times faster than a conventional freezer and therefore is an ideal preservation method for sportsmen who have neither the time or necessary facilities to freeze fish while in transit from one location to another.

Dry ice can be purchased in a variety of sizes and quantities. It is commonly manufactured for distributors in 10-inch square blocks, each weighing 54 pounds, but most traveling sportsmen prefer to have a workman, in an ice cream plant for example, saw off several inch-thick slabs for them, depending upon their needs.

A three-pound slab of dry ice measures one inch thick by five inches wide by seven inches long. In mid-1982 the going price was about 75 cents per pound.

To offer an illustration of the tremendous preservative capabilities of dry ice, consider this: A four-pound walleye wrapped in newspaper and placed between a couple of inch-thick slices of dry ice will be frozen rock solid in only six minutes!

The method generally accepted as best is to use an insulated cardboard box, wooden crate or camping cooler, with one or two slabs of dry ice first wrapped in newspaper and then placed in the middle of the storage container and the various fish packages surrounding the ice on all sides. I recommend that you use a ratio of approximately one pound of dry ice for every 10 pounds of fish. This quantity of dry ice will freeze the contents of the container within about 30 minutes, and in typical summer weather with the temperature around 80 degrees the ice should last about 20 hours before the supply needs to be replenished.

There are several precautions having to do with the use and handling of dry ice. For one, if you are using a tightly enclosed container such as a wooden crate or conventional camping cooler, some provision should be made for the escape of the carbon dioxide gas as the ice sublimates. With a cooler, leaving the drain valve open is usually sufficient; with a wooden box, drilling a few holes in the sides (before you leave home). Thick-walled, insulated cardboard boxes also are good bets, as are styrofoam camping coolers. In both cases the porous nature of the materials allows a natural breathing effect to take place through the walls of the container, even with the lid securely taped in place, so it is not necessary to be concerned about the gas.

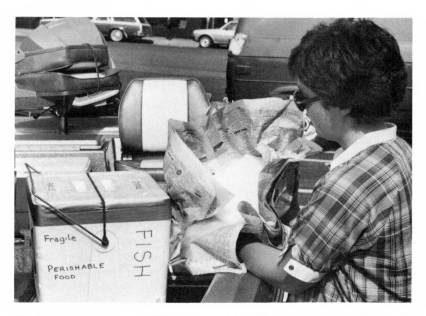

Dry ice can burn your fingers! Handle it carefully with rubber gloves, cradled in thick newspaper, or with a tool with wooden handles.

Also, fish must never be allowed to come in direct contact with dry ice. Wrap the fish first in plastic bags or freezer paper brought along for the purpose; then to further safeguard the fish, insert between the fish packages and the dry ice a quantity of wood shavings, excelsior, styrofoam "crumbles" or sawdust as filler packing materials. One or more of these materials are usually available free where you buy dry ice. If not, go to a newsstand and ask for day-old newspapers which you can shred and tear into strips for packing materials.

Never touch dry ice with your bare hands or you may receive a severe "burn." Use an old potholder to handle the stuff, or a thick piece of folded newspaper. Better yet, use rubber or leather gloves or a tool, such as tongs, with a wooden handle.

Finally, since the use of dry ice will see your fish quickly frozen, remember that it must remain that way since no meat should ever be allowed to defrost with the thought of re-freezing it. Have your various fish filleted or dressed and properly wrapped ahead of time in accordance with meal portions best suited to your family's needs. When you arrive home, simply transfer the frozen fish packages to your freezer.

If instead of driving you'll be flying by commercial carrier and then floatplane to some remote fishing camp, several methods can be used for transporting your catch home.

Most fishing camps will quick-freeze your fish as they are brought in each day. If a guide will be handling your fish, tell him ahead of time how you want your catch filleted or dressed and what quantities to freeze in each package. At the end of your visit, someone in camp will box up your fish in a plastic-coated or insulated cardboard container along with suitable packing materials. Then you can simply transport the fish home along with your luggage and other gear. Fish will stay solidly frozen in this manner for approximately 24 hours.

If the flight home should perchance exceed this 24-hour time limit, or there is an unexpected layover, check with the airport information desk and find out what freezer facilities are available for traveling sportsmen. If the airport itself doesn't offer this service, they can invariably suggest a particular hotel for your accommodations that customarily allows anglers to place boxes of fish overnight in their restaurant freezer.

Another alternative is to have the fishing-camp manager wrap and freeze your fish in the usual manner, properly box it and then a day or two after your departure ship it directly to your hometown via air-freight express. Boxes marked "Food...Perishable!" receive top priority and will arrive in your city within 24 hours. The going rate is about $25 per 100 pounds, which is very reasonable. For an additional charge the Customer Service divisions of many airlines will even deliver the fish right to your front door, but most anglers like to save a few bucks by driving to the airport to pick it up themselves.

2

Easy Ways to Dress and Fillet Fish

There is a seafood market in Akron, Ohio, where my brother Jeff worked for several years. It is not a very large operation compared to many others around the country, but it definitely has class.

A sign in the window advertises "the freshest fish in town," and anyone who has bought there can testify it is true. Except for shellfish or certain species that are pickled or smoked, many of the creatures are still alive and swimming around in tanks of water. The typical procedure sees a customer pick out the particular fish he wants, whereupon a member of the market's staff removes it from the tank with a dip net and dresses it right before the buyer's eyes.

The skill of these fillet artists is something to behold. It is like watching a team of master surgeons at work. Wandering eyes, in fact, may easily miss the whole show if they happen to be momentarily gazing off in some other direction. Those who do watch see a rapid series of zip-zip-slice-zip-slice motions, and the entire episode of dressing the fish is completed. Incredible as it may sound, the time we're talking about here is something around eight or ten seconds! When the fish are not filleted but only rough-dressed (scaled and with the head and innards removed), customers who walk out the front door with their neatly wrapped packages stalwartly claim they can actually feel the still-twitching musculature of the fish within the white paper. Now that is what I call "fresh fish," and no government agency investigating truth in advertising claims will ever close down the Akron seafood market.

As an aside, it's interesting that the highly skilled fillet and fish-dressing technicians at the above establishment invest awesome amounts of time sharpening their knives. Throughout the day, every minute or two, they can be seen touching up their blades on nearby stones, and then at night engaging in a more thorough sharpening so the knives will be scalpel-sharp for the following morning's work. This constant sharpening to maintain razor edges is obviously one reason why the workers are so proficient at their jobs and able to work so fast. But it also quickly nubs down the factory pre-formed bevels of the blades to such an extent that they soon are almost impossible to keep sharp, which is a state of affairs that begins to make itself known approximately every five weeks. Consequently, it's standard procedure that on the first of every month all the fillet knives in the shop are thrown away and brand new ones unboxed, which in turn will experience life spans of no longer than four weeks before they too are relegated to the trash pile.

It's always a real pleasure for me to watch professional cutters at work, like the experienced butchers in meat markets, who dress out very large and heavy carcasses seemingly with ease and with such precision that there is no waste whatever. I've seen a few big-game guides and outfitters do very creditable jobs on animals such as elk and moose, and now and then one is also likely to come across a deer hunter who really knows his stuff. Generally, mates on salt-water sportfishing boats are equally accomplished at their tasks. I've also watched a good number of trappers at work, who must be especially careful not to damage their valuable pelts.

Surprisingly, however, fresh-water fishermen are at the very bottom of the heap when it comes to knowledge or acquired skills regarding the cleaning of their catch. You don't have to take my word for it: just hang around the fish-cleaning shack of any popular marina or fishing camp for a few hours. Notice how nearly all the anglers show up with their catch in one hand and their knife in the other, but how virtually none of them have whetstones for touching up their blades. Notice how they lay a nice bass or walleye on the table and then give it a long, puzzled look, indicating that they don't have the foggiest idea how to attack the beast. Finally, when they're done, after an inordinate amount of time, notice the thoroughly botched-up, ragged, pitiful looking pieces of meat they walk away with, and how much good stuff, now ruined, goes unceremoniously into the trash can.

For shame! I say this not with a condescending air, because there is absolutely no reason to look upon the art of dressing or filleting fish as some mysterious secret or craft that can be mastered by only a few.

Cleaning fish is not a complicated or time-consuming matter. It is simply a physical, step-by-step operation anyone can learn in a few minutes. It falls into the same category of other simple mechanical tasks such as casting a lure, paddling a canoe or taking the exposed film out of your camera and putting in a fresh roll. Frequent practice, as in the case of any strictly manual labor, eventually will allow one to complete the job with a minimum investment of time and energy.

The first order of business is to prepare your work site. Some type of flat, hard surface is crucial to success. Any type of table standing at comfortable waist level (even your picnic table in the back yard) is ideal, or you can use boards or a sheet of plywood supported by sawhorses. Since any type of fish cleaning can be a bit messy, it's a good idea to work outdoors, or in your garage or basement during inclement weather. In other words, heed the old adage, "The devil hath no fury like a housewife confronted with fish scales clogging her kitchen sink."

A source of running water such as a garden hose is very helpful. This will allow you to wash slippery stuff from your hands and cutting surface, and also to rinse the finished fillets or dressed fish before transporting them to the kitchen. You'll need a plastic bag or garbage can for the cleanings. To keep flies and insects at bay during warm weather, fill a tin can with water, stir in several tablespoons of sugar, and pour it on the ground about 10 feet away from where you're working.

Finally, the presence of a good-quality fish fillet knife and sharpening stone is of paramount importance. Don't try to use a conventional meat knife or your hunting knife as both tools will destine your efforts to failure. What you want is a traditional fish fillet knife with a thin stainless steel blade 6½ to 7 inches long. These specialized knives differ from all others in that their blades are very flexible which allows them to be easily guided over, around and through various parts of the fish's anatomy.

The subject of knife sharpening has already been hashed over countless times in books and magazine articles so we needn't dwell upon the matter here. But I would emphasize that instead of waiting too long and then having to engage in a major, time-consuming sharpening effort, a much better tack is to merely keep the stone nearby and take three or four swipes across it every few minutes, even if the blade does not appear to require any immediate substantial work. This takes only a few seconds and ensures that the knife is continually at its best and ready to respond to your every command.

Filleting Bass, Walleyes and Trout

Now let's fillet a fish. For the purposes of illustration we'll use a 2½-pound largemouth bass (just the right "eating size," fishermen like to say, when they are unsuccessful at catching anything larger!). The method to be described is suitable for other elongate fish such as walleyes, trout, salmon, striped bass, most salt-water species and large panfishes such as jack perch and white bass.

I like to begin by washing the fish, rubbing it with a piece of toweling while thoroughly sloshing it with fresh water to remove surface mucus so the fish is no longer slippery and difficult to handle. Some anglers who are about to clean a large number of fish like to don a pair of lightweight cotton gardening gloves. Even when wet, such gloves ensure a firm grasp and also eliminate the otherwise inevitable feeling of "sandpaper hands" when the job is done.

First, lay the fish on its side so you are facing the belly and its head is pointing toward your right (directions are reversed for left-handers). With your left hand holding onto the fish near the tail, and the knife in your right hand, insert the tip of the knife into the fish's vent. Don't insert the knife more than ½ inch or you'll cut into the internal organs and have messy digestive matter spilling all over the place. With the tip of the blade in the vent, next open the abdominal and chest cavity by continuing the cut along the center of the belly all the way up to where the pelvic fins and gills are located.

Second, turn the fish around so its head is now facing left and you are facing its back or dorsal region. Holding onto the head of the fish with your left hand to steady it, slice down through the meat just behind the gills until you feel the blade stop against the backbone. If you make this downward slice slightly angular (front to back) in relation to the position of the fish, you'll retain the additional fillet meat along the dorsal region forward of the gills, yet also meet the vertical first slice you made behind the gills to eliminate the pectoral and pelvic fins from the side fillet.

Third, after you've sliced down through the side of the fish and felt the blade stop against the backbone, is to turn the fish slightly so the head is pointing toward you and the tail pointing away. Now, turn the blade sideways within the cut so the blade is laying flat against the backbone. Next, carefully guide the blade the entire length of the fish's body, making sure that it remains flat against the spine but is not permitted to cut any deeper than the dorsal fin along the back of the fish or the anal fin along the belly. Should the cut go deeper, there is risk of severing the spinal column and thereby damaging the fillet on the other side of the fish. This particular step is perhaps the most difficult for many anglers to master because slicing the fillet from the side of the body requires the cutting of ribs where they are attached to the backbone near the forward part of the body. Too often, amateurs using dull knives find they have to exert far more pressure to cut through the ribs than would be required with a sharp knife, and eventually the blade slips and tears the prime dorsal fillet meat rather than neatly slicing through it. So use a knife with a keen edge, and if a bit of resistance is encountered against the ribs, use a slight back-and-forth sawing motion rather than more force. Also, in removing the fillet meat from the side of the fish when moving in the direction of the tail, do not cut the fillet entirely free. Stop ½ inch before reaching the end of the fillet where the tail begins.

Fourth, lift the fillet and turn it over in the direction of the tail, skin-side down. Because you did not sever the fillet from the tail it will remain attached when you flip it over, almost like it is on a hinge. This allows you to remove the skin and attached scales all in one smooth operation while maintaining a secure hand-hold upon the rest of the carcass. Carefully slice down through the meat at the tail until you just barely begin to feel the blade of the knife touch the skin, then turn the blade flat so it can travel a course between the skin and fillet meat. Now, simultaneously begin pulling back on the carcass with your left hand while gently pushing the knife forward with the other and the meat should easily strip away from the skin with no waste whatever.

You now should have one perfectly formed fillet. It is entirely optional but many anglers use the tip of their knife blade to carefully remove the small segment of rib cage and abdominal wall skin remaining at the front of the fillet. Others prefer to leave this intact and remove it at the dinner table.

Turn the fish over and repeat the same procedure to remove the fillet from the other side, beginning with step two.

That's all! No muss, no fuming temper, no need to cut off the head of the fish, no need to remove the gills or innards or anything else. Much easier than any of that, as we've just seen, is to merely remove

2.

1. For elongate fishes like walleyes, trout or bass, begin the filleting procedure by slitting open the belly from the vent to the pelvic fins.

2. Next, slice down from the top of the back to the ventral cut. Angle the cut above the gills to retain the thick meat behind the head.

3. Now turn the blade flat against the backbone and guide the knife all the way to the tail to remove the slab of meat from the first side. Don't cut the meat free at the tail but stop just ½ inch away.

4. Then flop the fillet over on its self-made hinge and remove the skin and scales by guiding the knife blade as shown. Next, turn the fish over and repeat the same operation on the other side.

4.

5. The result is two professional-looking fillets ready for the kitchen. Some anglers like to remove the small segment of rib cage (on the opposite side of these fillets), while others prefer to save this operation until it's time to eat.

5.

the fillet slabs themselves from the sides of the fish, then throw the remaining carcass, still in one piece, into the trash can.

We should mention, however, that there are a few variations to the standard fillet technique described above. For one, many like to leave the skin on their fillets, preferring the crispy appearance this yields if the fish are fried. Leaving the skin on also is advised if the fish are to be broiled over charcoal, as the skin prevents the fillet meat itself from sticking to the grillwork. To produce fillets still in possession of their skins, first remove the fish's scales with a small scaling tool made for the purpose, or a dull knife blade, moving against the lay of the scales with short, brisk strokes of the hand. Then proceed

25

through steps one, two and three, severing the fillet completely free of the carcass at the tail rather than going through step four and the "hinge" treatment.

With an exceptionally large fish it is virtually impossible to cut through the ribs where they join the backbone when slicing the slab of meat away from the carcass as described in step three. In this situation, the recommended procedure is to go through steps one and two in the usual way. Then, in place of step three, make a shallow cut along the length of the backbone from the rear of the dorsal fin to just behind the head, and join it with the vertical cut made just behind the gills. This shallow cut, about one inch deep, will create a small flap of meat you can grab with your fingertips and gingerly lift as you use the tip of your blade to begin separating the fillet from around the rib cage along the side of the body. When the entire rib cage is eventually exposed, and thereby no longer attached to the slab of fillet meat, turn the blade flat against the backbone and proceed in slicing toward the tail to create the hinge in the usual fashion.

Learning how to properly fillet one's catch is the mark of an accomplished angler. Master the four-step method outlined here and you'll soon agree that there is no easier or more professional way.

Rough Dressing and Steaking

For many recipes, rough-dressed fish are more desirable than those which have been filleted. Rough dressing simply means cleaning the catch in such a manner that the meat is left on the skeleton, so that whole fish may be broiled, poached or filled with stuffing and baked.

Large (up to 15 pounds) and small fish both are suitable for rough dressing, and trout, bass, salmon, walleyes, striped bass, catfish, panfish and various salt-water species are most often given this treatment. There are several different ways of rough-dressing fish, or rather, several extremes one can go to, depending upon personal preferences. But the first three steps are the same, regardless.

First, completely scale the fish, using a scaling tool or the edge of a dull knife blade.

Second, with just the tip of your knife, slit open the ventral or belly region from the vent to the lower gill area and with your fingers remove the entrails.

1. To rough-dress fish, begin by using your knife blade, or a special tool made for the purpose, to remove the scales. Rub the blade or tool against the direction that the scales are attached, from tail to head.

1.

2. Prop the fish up on its belly and remove the head. Note how the cut curves to retain the meat along the backbone just behind the head, but then swings out and away to go around the gill structure.

2.

3. With a single slice, now remove the vent and lower fin.

3.

4. Rough-dressing a fish takes only two or three minutes. Many anglers like to leave the tails on, because when fried to crispy perfection they taste like potato chips. When cooked, the dorsal fin easily pulls away to be discarded.

4.

Third, run the edge of a teaspoon or your thumbnail along the spinal cord inside the body. This will have the effect of breaking open the blood vessel that is closely attached, so that its contents may be rinsed away with clean water. Otherwise this vessel, the cardinal vein, may impart an objectionable flavor to the fish.

Some people like to remove the head. The easiest way is by propping the fish up on its belly and cutting downward, through the neck region. Make this cut as close as possible behind the head, but as the knife blade is traveling downward swing the blade out so that it goes around the gill flaps. This maneuver serves a dual purpose: it allows the quick and easy removal of not only the entire gill structure but also the pelvic and pectoral fins lying just below the gills, yet allows you to retain the thick portion of meat just behind the head.

However, some like to leave the head intact, feeling it offers a more pleasing appearance on the dinner platter. This is especially the case when baking a large trout, salmon or striped bass. In this situation, prop the fish up on its back, and beginning in the lower gill area remove the entire filament and raker assemblies while leaving the gill covers in place.

At this stage, some like to use the tip of their knife blade to cut out the dorsal fin, adipose fin, ventral fin, or any other appendages, including the tail, but this is entirely optional. I personally like to leave these fins on because it looks much nicer when the fish is served whole. The tails on panfish, when crispy brown, are very tasty and just like potato chips.

Steaking fish such as salmon is accomplished by first rough-dressing the fish. Then, prop it up on its belly and make vertical, inch-thick slices to produce the steaks.

Steaking fish is quite easy and merely consists of one additional step after completing all of the above. Prop the fish up on its belly and slice all the way down at intervals to produce inch-thick steaks for broiling or baking. If your fillet knife seems to meet too much resistance when it contacts the spinal cord, wiggle the blade "just a hair" to allow it to pass between the vertebrae of the backbone rather than contacting them squarely.

Finally, we should mention one part of the fish's anatomy that often is overlooked by anglers: the cheek meat. Admittedly, cheeks are only worth the trouble of removing from fish of five pounds or larger. They are located just behind the eye region and you can easily locate them by pressing with your fingertip and feeling for a soft spot. Use the tip of your knife blade to encircle the cheek with a shallow cut, and pluck it out. These cheeks are about the sizes of big marbles and are extremely tender and flavorful, although you'll have to accumulate a good quantity of them in your freezer before there will be enough for a meal.

Filleting Pike, Muskies and Pickerel

For years, members of the *Esox* genus have been regarded as poor foodfishes, and this is unfortunate because just the opposite is true. They are excellent.

We're talking here about northern pike, the several different musky subspecies and both the chain pickerel and grass pickerel.

The main reason these fish have poor reputations in the kitchens of North American anglers has very little to do with their flavor or the tender texture of their flesh. It is because the danged things can be quite difficult to clean (for those who don't know how), and that also makes them quite difficult to eat. The culprit is the complicated structure of their spinal columns.

Unlike other fresh-water fish that have a backbone and rib cage compartment, pike, muskies and pickerel have a somewhat different anatomy. They have the same backbone and rib cage design as bass, walleyes and other fish, but also a secondary, floating skeletal system that runs from their necks to their dorsal fins. Anglers usually refer to these additional bones as Y-bones because that describes exactly what they look like. By any description, the bones are downright pesky

Here, Bill Weiss admires a nice pike taken in northern Manitoba. Pike, muskies and chain pickerel are excellent foodfishes, but many shy away from eating them because of the pesky Y-bones that are difficult to remove when eating.

to remove when dressing a fish, and just as troublesome to pick one by one out of the meat while you're eating.

First, either scrub the fish or scald it briefly, depending upon where you are and what conveniences you have on hand. This removes the body slime these species possess, and also slightly loosens their securely attached scales. If the slime is not removed, pike, muskies and pickerel can be very slippery, which increases the chances of doing a sloppy cleaning job with your knife or even accidentally poking your own hide.

To scald any of the species, dunk the entire fish into a large pot of water that has almost but not quite reached the boiling point. If it's a big fish which, because of its length, you won't be able to get into even a big pot, hang the fish by the mouth outside somewhere and pour the scalding water over it. If you're in camp and heating a pot of water would be impractical, use any kind of stiff bristle brush, paper towels, or coarse fabric rag such as terrycloth to vigorously rub the sides of the fish for a few minutes.

Second, now that the fish is no longer slippery and difficult to handle, begin the filleting procedure by propping the fish up on its belly. The best method for me is to hold the fish upright by the head with my left hand, with the fillet knife in my right hand.

Third, carefully cut straight down into the meat, just behind the head, until you feel the blade come to an abrupt halt when it reaches the backbone.

Fourth, turn the knife flat and run the edge of the blade all the way back along the top of the backbone until you reach the beginning of the dorsal fin. At this point, simply curve the knife blade up and finish the cut so you can lift out the first long fillet. This is the prime cut from any pike, musky or pickerel and it is 100 percent boneless.

Fifth, lay the fish on its side, with the now-exposed backbone facing toward you. You will easily be able to see the spinal column running lengthwise through the center of the fish, and you'll notice as well a row of Y-bones, just the tips of them exposed, lying on each side of the backbone. It's a simple matter, then, to run the tip of your knife blade close along the outside (skin-side) edge of these bones. The cut need only be about ½ inch in depth and should run horizon-

1.

1. It's easy to fillet pike, muskies and chain pickerel so that all Y-bones are removed. First, remove the dorsal fillet in one simple step by cutting straight down behind the head, turning the blade flat against the top of the spine and guiding the blade all the way to the beginning of the dorsal fin where it is then separated from the body.

2.

2. Next, lift up a flap of skin just behind the gills. You'll see the protruding Y-bones. With the tip of your knife, run the blade between the Y-bones and the side meat. When the knife reaches the dorsal fin area, sever the fillet.

tally all the way from the back of the head to the beginning of the dorsal fin. Now, with the fish still lying on its side, make two vertical slices, one just behind the head and the other where the dorsal fin begins. Cut all the way down until the knife blade touches the spinal column. By doing this, you'll have created a small flap of meat. By lifting up this loose flap (the Y-bones remain underneath) and carefully cutting some more, gradually working your way toward the belly, the remainder of the side fillet will eventually be released. Now, flop the fish over and do the same thing on the other side to obtain that fillet.

Sixth, remove the tail fillets, on both sides of the fish, the same way you'd ordinarily fillet a bass. That is, with the fish lying on its side, lay your knife blade flat against the exposed backbone and slice all the way to the tail, continually keeping the blade as close as possible to the backbone to minimize waste.

The whole thing may sound complicated, but if you look at the step-by-step pictures everything should come into clear focus. With a little practice you should be able to fillet a pike, musky or pickerel of any size in only a few minutes.

You should now have five entirely boneless fillets lying before you: the dorsal fillet, two side-body fillets and two tail fillets. The remainder of the fish carcass will be intact, since there has been no need to gut the fish, cut out the gills, or anything like that.

There is one *last* step, and that is to skin the fillets. Do this easily, the same way you'd skin fillets from any species of fish, by laying each fillet skin-side down. At the closest end of the fillet you're working on, cut into the meat just where it joins the edge of skin underneath.

3. Remove the tail fillet, next, in the same way you'd finish removing the fillet from a bass or any other fish. Finally, strip off the skin and scales in the usual manner.

4. The end product is five fillets that are all entirely bone-free. Note how the fish carcass remains intact, as there has been no need to remove the head, entrails or anything else.

This cut will create a little knob of flesh that you can hold securely with your fingertips while you guide the blade the rest of the way. I like to hold the edge of the knife at about a 20-degree angle to the cutting board and push it the length of the fillet with a very slight back-and-forth sawing motion, which causes the skin to separate cleanly with no loss of meat.

Pike and muskies are two species which, because of their generally large sizes, are ideal candidates for cheek removal. The other part of a pike, musky or pickerel you should never throw away is the liver. You can fry it with onions like you would calves' liver, but many anglers prefer to mash it up into a delectable spread (check any cookbook for many liver paté recipes) for crackers or sandwiches. Or, you can dice the liver finely and add it to turkey or gamebird stuffings.

Of course, due to the Y-bones in the aforementioned species, pike and such are not really suitable for rough dressing or steaking, unless you're willing to pick out countless bones by hand at the dinner table. But if you try the new filleting method I've outlined here, I guarantee you'll be pleased. And I'll bet your family will be prodding you to go pike or musky fishing more often!

Dressing and Skinning Catfish

Catfish won't win any beauty contests, but on the table they are just as flavorful as some gamefish species, sometimes more so.

Generally, small catfish and bullheads are best fried or broiled whole, while larger fish are better filleted or steaked.

First, remove the tough skin which is not unlike leathery shark

33

1. **1.** To clean a catfish it is first necessary to remove the tough, shark-like hide. Begin by making a shallow cut behind the head and down the sides, going around the gills.

2. **2.** Now grab the skin with pliers and pull back. You may have to employ the "Armstrong" method. If the skin tears away, grab it some place else and continue pulling. Some anglers use pliers for this.

3. **3.** The skin should come off like a very tough banana skin. Then, continue cleaning the cat by the method of your choice. You can slice off fillet slabs, rough dress the fish for baking or cut thick steaks.

hide. Lay the fish belly-down, and with your knife blade make a very shallow "scoring" cut just behind the head and then down and around the gill areas.

Second, use the "Armstrong" method of pulling off the skin, so named because with some cats, particularly the larger ones, a good deal of muscle power may be required. Some anglers, in fact, to increase their leverage, like to drive a large nail through the cat's head to hold the fish securely to the cutting board. You'll need some type of pliers for this step, and they should have strong jaws with teeth so the skin does not slip out. Now, by merely pulling on the skin in the direction of the tail, it should begin coming away much like a banana peel. You may occasionally have to make a judicious slice here and there with your knife blade, especially around the belly region, to ensure that continued pulling on the skin does not result in large chunks of flesh tearing away.

Once the cat is skinned, other procedures depend upon how the fish is to be prepared for the table. If you'll be frying fish, broiling or baking, and want slab fillets, remove them as you would from a bass. Or, you can steak the fish, after first removing the head, tail and various fins.

Small cats, up to 1½ pounds, are usually best when rough-dressed, in which case you'll want to remove the head, gill structure, fins and of course the insides.

Dressing and Filleting Panfish

A good number of my most memorable fish dinners have taken place when the guests of honor were bluegills, sunfish, perch, crappies, rock bass, white bass and similar species.

Often, I like to fry them whole, in rough-dressed form. To rough-dress panfish follow the same steps described earlier for rough-dressing small trout, bass, walleyes and the like. I practically always leave the tails on panfish and eat them at the table. Also leave the dorsal fin intact, as it pulls away easily after the fish is cooked, but remove the other fins.

Many anglers think of filleting fish only in terms of larger specimens, believing there isn't enough meat on panfish to attempt this

1. **1.** Experts can fillet about three panfish per minute. Step one is making an angular slice just behind the head.

2. **2.** With just the tip of your knife, now slice down to but not through the backbone and continue the cut all the way to the back of the dorsal fin.

3. **3.** When you reach the back of the dorsal fin, push the tip of the blade all the way through to the ventral side and then continue the slice until the meat separates at the tail.

4. Next, using the tip of your knife blade to follow the lateral line, remove the fillet chunk along the back-bone and down to the tail.

5. The fillet should pop right out. Then remove the skin and scales in the usual manner.

6. No muss, no fuss. The body of the panfish remains completely intact with sep-arated fillets nearby. Each fillet is about the size of a jumbo shrimp.

with them. Not so, provided you use a special filleting technique designed solely for these smaller species.

I have to give credit to my friend Bill Gressard of Ravenna, Ohio, for this super way of filleting panfish. It may sound incredible, but I have seen Bill fillet a couple hundred panfish in only 1½ hours! After filleting your first 50 bluegills or sunfish (or other species) you should be able to do about two per minute. Gressard can fillet three per minute and watching his quick hands at work is like witnessing the artful moves of a Vegas blackjack dealer.

First, with your fillet knife cut down to but not through the backbone, just behind the head, with the fish lying on its side.

Second, insert the tip of the knife just behind the head and work it down the side of the dorsal fin, making sure that the knife does not cut any deeper than the rib cage.

Third, as soon as you reach the rear of the dorsal fin, push the tip of the knife all the way through to the ventral side and with the knife edge sliding over the backbone, continue to the tail and cut the fillet free.

Fourth, with the tip of the knife riding over the upper edge of the rib cage, follow the lateral line, gradually lowering the cut until it meets the ventral area where you pushed the knife all the way through. The fillet should literally "pop" right out.

Fifth, remove the skin from the fillet as if filleting a bass or trout, by holding the tail section firmly and sliding the blade between the skin and the fillet.

Sixth, flop the fish and repeat the procedure on the other side.

Using this method, there is no need to scale the fish, gut them, cut off the heads, or remove any of the fins. Each fillet from an average eight-inch bluegill will be about the size of a jumbo shrimp, or even larger if taken from panfishes such as crappies or jack perch.

There are numerous ways these mini-fillets can be prepared for the table, but first prize goes to Bill Gressard's beer batter recipe, which I'll describe in the next chapter.

3

Failsafe Fish Cookery

Whenever I happen to be perusing the hoards of fish recipes that commonly appear in sportsmen's magazines or books, for the purpose of experimenting with them and then adding the ones I like to my own permanent file, I sometimes begin feeling paranoid, like I'm the greatest nonconformist in the world. What I mean is, I find it very difficult to go along with the apparently never-ending trend of camouflaging the flavor of fish with assorted marinades, tomato sauces, mustard preparations and exotic spices which you have to special order from some forgotten corner of the world at a price that would gag an Arab sheik. In my mind, the real flavor of properly prepared fish is truly exquisite, and the many different species do not, in any manner of speaking, have to be served *au costume* in order to be edible.

It is true that fish flavors can vary enormously between species. But all fish are unique in the sense that unlike red meat, fish flesh possesses little or no connective tissue and therefore always cooks quickly and if not overdone (a cardinal sin) is always tender, even though the flesh of certain species is of a coarser grain and to the palate seems more dense in texture. In all cases, however, it is the predator species—the gamefish and panfish—which are the most flavorful, and those which come from clean, cold water are doubly so. Yet lesser fish species—the scavengers, sometimes referred to as "rough fish," such as suckers, carp, sheepshead and certain of the catfish clan—also can afford tasty dining if handled properly. Catfish can be baked, broiled, fried or used in the creation of robust chowders and stews, while the others are generally best either smoked or pickled.

Additionally, the most eventful fish dinners are predominantly those which see the fish served as soon as possible after they have been caught. Fish must never undergo an aging process, as they are never more fresh, tender and flavorful than shortly after they have been re-moved from the water. The very best fish dinners, then, are predict-ably those served along the water's edge at noon, perhaps later when boats have taken their nightly resting places in mooring slips, or at home shortly after the catch has been duly admired and applauded by all.

Yet in any of these situations there is the distinct likelihood that the angler/cook will not have on hand numerous spices or other fixin's that are not common staples in the kitchen cupboard. Nor is it likely, after a long day on the water, that he will have the desire, energy or enthusiasm to wade laboriously through a complex recipe. I have seen many recipes requiring as many as 15 different ingredients and eight mixing or cooking steps, culminating in something for which one might pay upwards of $20 a plate in some chic French restaurant, but that tastes nothing like fresh fish. With all due respect to authors who deal with this subject, that is about as ludicrous as taking a shower while wearing a raincoat.

Therefore, although I will indeed later in this chapter offer a mod-est selection of just slightly gussied-up recipes on behalf of any read-ers who may consider themselves budding gourmets, the vast majority of cooking suggestions related during the meanwhile are quite simple. As fish cookery should be, these recipes require a minimum of readily available ingredients and a brief cooking time, and one need not have been schooled by the Master Chef at the Hotel Quinta de Penha de Franca in Funchal, Madeira, in order to place before his family a de-lightful and memorable meal. Admittedly, however, every suggestion does carry a certain element of risk, in that guests who have previous-ly sampled such repasts on your part may make a habit of trampling each other as they rush to the table. Or, there may be a consensus that you be given full charge of all future kitchen duties, and that is something that can very seriously cut into one's fishing time.

Fried Fish

Frying, though probably the easiest and most popular method of pre-paring fish, is best suited to only certain species. In the cases of other fish, because of the unique features of their meats, baking or broiling may be much better than frying.

Just a few of the particular fish species that are ideal for frying include all of the black bass species and true basses such as stripers (provided that individual fish do not exceed three pounds in weight), all of the panfish species (such as perch, bluegills and crappies), walleyes and saugers up to five pounds, grayling of all sizes, and brook trout, brown trout, rainbow trout, cutthroat trout and golden trout that weigh less than three pounds.

If you try to "fry up" a big carp, salmon, musky, whitefish or char, be prepared to spend the late evening hours imbibing liberal dosages of Bromo Seltzer.

A cast-iron skillet evenly disperses heat for uniform frying. The right temperature for the cooking oil is imperative. Use an inexpensive thermometer that clips to the side of the pan to monitor the temperature.

Whatever the species to be fried, I suggest the use of a heavy, cast-iron skillet. Frypans of steel or aluminum do not evenly disperse the heat over the metal's entire cooking surface; as a result, hot spots often develop here and there, sometimes causing part of the fish to scorch.

Vegetable cooking oils are far better for frying fish than oils made of animal fats (an exception is bacon drippings) which may impart undesirable flavors. Buy the best available–Wesson Oil or Crisco Oil. You worked hard for your fish, so don't risk sacrificing any smidgen of their goodness merely to save a dime or two on the cooking oil.

The perfect temperature for frying fish is just shy of smoking hot, or around 370 degrees. This is easily achieved and maintained when cooking over an electric or gas range or using a gasoline or propane campstove. When cooking over a campfire, you'll have to be more careful. Make sure there is an ample supply of kindling nearby with which to keep the fire well stoked, as that guarantees a plentiful number of coals in reserve that can be raked into the cooking area as needed.

In order to maintain the suggested 370-degree temperature, I use a cooking thermometer that clips onto the side of the frypan. These cost only a buck and are available in any grocery store. If the meal is being prepared at lakeside, an accurate way of measuring the heat is by dropping a small cube of bread into the hot oil. When it begins to bubble, dance around the skillet and turn brown around the edges, the oil is ready.

When frying fish I always try to keep the fillets or whole fish very cold before they are slipped into the cooking oil. The reaction between the hot oil and cold fish puts a sealing crust on the fish which prevents the inner flesh from absorbing the oil and becoming soggy and greasy tasting.

Also make sure that you place only *one* piece of fish into the skillet at a time and then wait a full minute before adding the next piece. Adding all of the cold fish all at once will drastically lower the temperature of the cooking oil and this in turn requires a much longer cooking time and results in the fish becoming dried out rather than remaining moist and flaky.

Whenever possible use a spatula to turn the fish, rather than a fork which often tears the fish apart or punctures the crust accidently. When the fish are to be turned, it is important they be turned only once! Flip-flopping them back and forth numerous times will break the sealing crust and allow the inner flesh to absorb the cooking oil.

When the fish are brown and crisp around the edges, and light golden everywhere else, they are done. Carefully remove them from the pan and allow them to drain on paper toweling before serving. If your cooking facilities allow for it, present the fish on a pre-heated platter to keep them hot throughout the entire meal, or at least cover them with foil.

If it sounds like I'm neurotically fussy about these various steps in frying fish, you're right! Because adding up all of these little things invariably means the difference between fried fish that are of truly high quality and those that are greasy and "bluuuck" tasting. Nine times

One key to fried fish that is not greasy tasting is using very cold fish, to produce a sealing crust. Another important thing is adding only one fish at a time to the pan; adding all the fish at once drastically lowers the temperature of the cooking oil.

in ten it is not the particular batter, mix or other ingredients that determine the end result, but the care and loving with which each of the various steps is implemented.

It is very likely that there are as many different fish-frying recipes as there are anxious anglers who like to stand around and pester a cook for "field test" samples. My own file alone contains what I consider the 87 best frying recipes of the hundreds I've tried. But this is not simply a one-recipe-after-another cookbook, so I'll only relate here the special few that my dinner guests have asked for most often over the past 15 years.

For any of the bass species the most exceptional recipe I have ever tasted was relayed to me long ago by my friend Inky Davis, a professional guide at the famous Santee-Cooper lakes in South Carolina. The recipe involves buttermilk. To tell the truth, drinking buttermilk straight makes me choke, but when it is used in cooking it can't be tasted and yet does a yeoman's job of bringing out the subtle, distinctive flavors of largemouth, smallmouth and spotted bass.

Buttermilk Bass
2 pounds bass fillets
1 quart buttermilk
Aunt Jemima Buttermilk Pancake Flour
cooking oil

Place the fillets in a deep glass bowl, completely cover them with the buttermilk, cover the bowl and let the fish soak for one hour. Briefly shake each fillet to remove any excess milk, dredge them in the pancake flour and then place one fillet at a time in bubbling hot cooking oil as described earlier. Serves four.

Buttermilk Bass is rated first, but Savory Bass is in close contention. Again, only a very few ingredients are required, but that shouldn't be too surprising because many of the best things in life are extremely simple.

Savory Bass
2 pounds bass fillets
1 cup flour
4 tablespoons Lawry's Seasoned Salt
cooking oil

Thoroughly mix the flour and Lawry's salt in a brown paper bag. Add two fillets at a time and shake the bag until they are well coated and then slip them into the frypan and let them sizzle to perfection. Serves four.

Every year my friend Bill Gressard supplies local restaurants with thousands of panfish from his private lake. I have added to my file his superb recipe for bluegills or sunfish. It's a beer batter recipe, but that should not discourage teetotalers from enjoying this special meal because the small amount of alcohol evaporates during the cooking process. (See Chapter 2 for Bill's quick-and-easy method of filleting panfish.)

Bill Gressard's Beer Batter Bluegills
2 pounds bluegill fillets
1 cup pancake flour
1 egg
1 cup beer
1 teaspoon salt

Mix the flour, egg, beer and salt until they are thoroughly blended into a moderately thick batter. Dip the fillets into the batter, shake off any excess, then drop them one at a time into hot cooking oil. They are done in about two minutes or when golden brown. Drain the fish on paper towels and then, if you like, eat them with your fingers. Serves four.

Although the above recipe originally was devised for use with small panfish fillets, it also is outstanding when used with larger fillets from bass, walleyes, striped bass, pike, muskies and other species, provided the fillets from such fish are reduced to acceptable sizes before frying.

Panfish can also be fried whole (photos showing how to dress them appear in Chapter 2). For bluegills and sunfish, not much can be done to improve upon their flavor other than shaking them in a paper bag containing white flour and then sliding them into a frypan with a good amount of melted bacon drippings. For crappies, use Shake 'n Bake, cracker crumbs, Frying Magic Mix or cornmeal.

Perch are panfish species that provide royal fare when fried in butter. They'll arrive at crispy perfection if you merely scale them, fillet them (leave the skin on) and dust them lightly with flour. Care must be exercised to ensure that the butter (or margarine) is not allowed to burn or scorch, which is exactly what will happen as a result of "clarifying" or the settling out of the milk solids in the butter as the temperature rises. Remedy the problem by stirring in two tablespoons of cooking oil or bacon drippings as the butter or margarine is melting.

Catfish, especially whole bullheads or fillets from channel cats, also do well when fried in butter. Dredging them first with flour is a favorite method. But for a pleasant change of pace, try dunking them in beaten eggs and then rolling them in well-ground potato chip crumbs. Or, dip whole skinned catfish (small ones, weighing less than a pound) in a mixture of beaten eggs and milk and then roll them thoroughly in a mixture of flour and dry bread crumbs before adding them to the frypan. As with all fish, quickly remove them from the heat when the flesh flakes easily.

There is no better way to fry trout or walleyes than that used by Indian guides in Canada and outfitters who pack clients in by horse to remote alpine lakes. Simply shake the walleye fillets or whole, dressed trout in a paper bag containing white flour and then drop them into bubbling hot cooking oil. Walleyes and trout are reputed among millions of anglers to be the most flavorful fish species, and those who use anything other than flour (and perhaps just a touch of salt) should be branded for what they are: criminals.

Smaller pike and muskies are usually released to grow larger as it takes either of these toothy fishes upwards of 25 years to reach trophy sizes. But if times are hard, or it has been a long while between fish dinners, both species can be fried to delectable goodness. For best results, I rely upon any of the bass or panfish recipes listed earlier.

As a way of adding exciting new touches to any of the previous recipes, without adding ingredients that unduly compete with the natural flavors of the fish themselves, try substituting whole wheat flour for white flour. Or, as the fish are frying, sprinkle them lightly with dried onion flakes. Or just as they are about done, douse them gently with a bit of lemon juice. Or add a little coarse black pepper to the flour or other dry mix.

Unless you've planned ahead and made more fish than your crew can possibly eat at one sitting, it's not likely there will be any left over. But if there are, for heaven's sake don't feed them to the cat. Wrap the remaining fish in plastic or foil and store it for up to three days in your refrigerator or camp cooler.

One way to re-serve the fish, perhaps for a light lunch, is to place the fillets in a skillet (add no oil), cover, and let them warm on very low heat for 12 to 15 minutes, turning them only once.

However, what I like most is to top each piece of fish with a slice of cheese (American, Swiss, or mild cheddar), place each fillet in a sesame seed bun, wrap each sandwich separately in foil, and place in a 350-degree oven for ½ hour or until the fish is steaming hot and the cheese melted. If you are in camp, set the foil packages at the edge of your campfire coals for 45 minutes, turning them frequently.

Baked Fish

Almost any fish that is over three pounds in weight usually tastes better when baked or broiled than when panfried. The reason is that attempts to fry thick slabs of fish in hot cooking oil usually result in the edges and outside surfaces of the flesh becoming too well done and the insides not being cooked at all. Also, some fish species have darker, more oily flesh than others, and dunking them in cooking oil does them no justice whatever.

Just a few of the species that are ideal for baking include steelhead, brown trout, rainbow trout, lake trout, pike, muskies, salmon, striped bass and large black bass.

You can bake these fishes whole with their heads, tails and fins intact but with their gills and insides removed, or you can fillet them and bake the slabs of meat. Or, after the fish have been scaled and rough-dressed they can be sliced vertically into inch-thick steaks. These approaches involve personal preference more than anything else, but baking techniques do vary slightly with different species.

White-fleshed or non-oily fish such as bass, pike, muskies, walleyes and catfish should be wrapped in foil for most of their required baking time. Their flesh is less moist and the foil will retain steam and juices so the fish do not become dried out as they bake. Dotting each whole fish, fillet or steak with little pieces of butter, before the foil is closed, is a good idea. Also, rub the inside of the body cavity or sprinkle the fillets or steaks with just a bit of lemon juice.

Darker-fleshed or oily fish such as many of the trout and salmon species do not require a foil enclosure. As these fish bake, the oils and juices exuding from their flesh offer a continual basting effect. However, with these fish, the use of lemon juice is not recommended. Instead, for those particular species that have dark red or fatty flesh, and are to be baked whole, insert into the body cavity a couple of quartered apple slices (which are discarded when the fish is served).

The best way to bake fish is to first pre-heat your oven to 400 degrees, then place the whole fish (best profile up), steaks or fillet slabs —if required, in aluminum foil—in a shallow pan.

For generations, the baking time for all fish was erroneously described as "so many minutes per pound." The problem with this was that it too often resulted in fish either overcooked or undercooked;

for example, an eight-pound pike and an eight-pound bass would both be baked for the same length of time, but since the pike was long and slim in shape and the bass relatively short and stocky, the pike would predictably come out overcooked and dry and the bass would be raw.

It was James Beard, the renowned chef and cookbook author, who cleared the air.

"Forget about how much the fish weighs," Beard advised. "Bake it for 10 minutes per inch of thickness as measured at the thickest part of the fish."

This is excellent advice, yet every angler must temper his own efforts with flexibility and good judgment because there are wide variances in the efficiency capabilities of home ranges; gas ranges, more than electrics, are notoriously fickle. So after I have estimated the fish to be about two-thirds done I usually begin poking it a bit to see if the

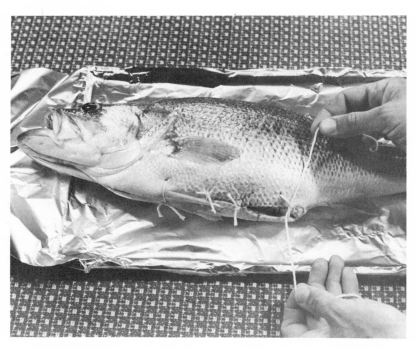

Baking is an excellent way to prepare fish weighing over three or four pounds. Bake them 10 minutes per inch of thickness as measured at the thickest part of the fish. Here, the author has filled a six-pound bass with stuffing and is closing the body opening with cotton string.

flesh is cooked and separates easily into large flakes. As little as four minutes of overcooking may begin to diminish the fish's tenderness.

Just before removing the fish from the oven, when they are almost done, I turn back the foil and slide them under the broiler for a couple of minutes to achieve a light brown finish on top. However, this is not necessary with oily fish not covered with foil as the continual basting effect will already have given them a bronzed appearance.

When baking fish whole, many anglers like to insert stuffing into the body cavity. You can use any that are to your liking, even ones customarily intended for use with Thanksgiving turkey or gamebirds such as pheasants. But I would offer a few additional tips. Go very light on the sage and other spices, as they may tend to compete with or even overwhelm the flavor of the fish, which rightfully should be the main attraction. If the whole fish to be stuffed is one of the white-fleshed, non-oily species such as bass, add just a bit more water than the stuffing recipe calls for. If the fish is a red-fleshed, oily species such as salmon, use slightly less water. Also, do not fill the body cavity more than two-thirds full as the stuffing will expand as it cooks. The body cavity can then be secured with standard meat skewers or lacing pins, or you can sew it closed with a large needle and cotton string to prevent the stuffing from spilling out.

Two stuffing recipes specifically intended for use with baked fish are as follows.

Mushroom Stuffing
2 cups dried bread crumbs
½ cup chopped onion
4 tablespoons butter
½ cup canned mushrooms
1 tablespoon tarragon
1 teaspoon grated lemon rind
dry white wine

In a deep skillet, sauté the onions in the butter until they are clear. Add the can of mushrooms along with the juice from the can and continue cooking over low heat for five to eight minutes. Turn off the heat and stir in the tarragon, lemon rind and bread crumbs, adding the wine as necessary to make the stuffing moist. Insert in body cavity and close.

Rice Stuffing
½ cup butter
1 onion, minced
1 cup minced celery
2 cups cooked Minute Rice
½ cup mushrooms (optional)
½ teaspoon sage
¼ teaspoon black pepper
½ teaspoon thyme
¼ teaspoon salt

In a deep skillet sauté the onions and celery in the butter. Add the mushrooms and cook slowly an additional five minutes. Add the spices. Thoroughly mix in the cooked rice, then insert the stuffing into the fish.

Finally, regarding baked fish, if you're in camp and don't have the facilities for baking fish in a conventional oven, here's a nifty way for baking them in foil. Lay out a 14-inch square of heavy duty foil for each angler. In the center of the foil lay two strips of bacon, then on top lay a thick fish fillet or steak. On top of the fish lay a slice of onion, several potato slices, salt and pepper to taste, followed by two more strips of bacon on top. Fold the edges of the foil tightly so no steam can escape and then bury each package in the coals for about 20 minutes. Each eager diner will require no more than a fork because he can turn back the edges of the foil and enjoy his complete meal from the makeshift plate.

Broiled Fish

One of the most exciting lake trout dinners I have ever feasted upon was a spur of the moment thing, and it required no ingredients or cooking utensils of any kind. Jimmy Bartok and I were fishing a northern Manitoba lake and we had three nice fish in the boat, all in the six-pound range. Jimmy is a Cree Indian from the nearby Pukatawagan Reservation, and he had been teaching me the art of deep-water jigging.

When the noon hour arrived, Bartok suggested we broil one of the fish and then pointed the bow of the boat toward a handy shoreline. Next he took one of the lakers and split it lengthwise down the center of the back from head to tail, leaving the belly section intact as a sort of connecting hinge. Then he removed the fish's ribs, backbone, head and innards with his knife and that left a thick slab of meat about 12 inches wide by 20 inches long. Meanwhile, I set to the task of building a robust fire from dry birch.

Then Jimmy fetched from the boat a short length of oak board that I noticed had four equally spaced holes drilled in it. Next, he hiked to a nearby willow tree and from a green branch cut four short pegs. With that, the fish was "tacked" to the oak board, held in place by the pegs first pierced through the meat and then wedged tightly into the holes. Jimmy completed the effort in not much more time than I have taken to describe here, and then the board was propped up at an angle beside the licking flames.

Trout are excellent when broiled whole, or in the case of large fish, in steaks or fillets. These rainbows and goldens were caught in Montana and very shortly will find themselves over a bed of white-ash embers.

Several times the board had to be re-positioned so that all parts of the slab of fish would be adequately exposed to the fire. As that trout broiled, releasing into the air indescribably delicious aromas, I began to understand how our ancestors were able to survive without the scads of equipment most modern sportsmen find necessary to have in their keep.

When the trout had a whiskey-brown finish, Jimmy said it was ready. We ate with our fingers, picking large chunks of flaky, hot meat from the carcass, popping them into our mouths, and now and then sipping ice-cold water from the clean wilderness lake. It was the most primitive dining adventure I have ever experienced, and yet one of the most enchanting.

Frying, baking and other cooking methods are products of civilized man, but broiling probably dates back to the first uses of fire, when some cave dweller accidently discovered that meat which had fallen into the fire tasted better than that eaten raw. Today, the principles of broiling are about the same as they have always been; in most cases, we simply use more modern equipment.

From my experience, it is better to broil large fish rather than small ones, and it is also better, in most cases, to use fillet slabs or steaks rather than whole fish. Therefore, large bass, trout, pike, muskies and similar species are the most desirable.

With species that have red, oily flesh, little is required other than to begin broiling them, as it is difficult to make a mistake; the fatty nature of the flesh affords the necessary properties to keep the meat from drying out. With species possessing a more delicate flesh, such as bass, it is best to brush them frequently with melted butter or bacon drippings to prevent the meat from burning or becoming too dry.

When using the broiler in your oven at home, the fish should be placed approximately three or four inches from the heat source and the oven door left slightly ajar.

When broiling fish over an open fire, the technique differs slightly. Charcoal can be used, but better are hardwood chunks that have burned down to glowing embers. Grates and grills are *verboten* because the fish, as they cook, will often break and fall through the wide spaces between the steel rods. Better is some type of fine wire mesh grill in which the space between the individual steel rods or woven wire is no more than ¾ inch. Better still are those flat basket affairs with a long handle, which open up to allow the fish to be inserted between two wire grills. The advantage of this is that the fish can be easily turned without accidently incurring damage.

In any of the above cases, place the fillets or steaks within an inch of the heat for the first two minutes (one minute on each side) to sear the meat slightly and seal in the juices. Then raise the grill about six inches higher to complete the cooking. Poke the fish occasionally to see if they are done; the meat should have a dark golden crust and yet be moist inside.

A few other tips are worth mentioning. When broiling fish in an oven, I remove the skin from fillets (but not from steaks) and set the meat on a sheet of aluminum foil to prevent it from sticking to the broiler pan. I also remove the skin from fillets when cooking over coals and I smear the grill with vegetable oil to prevent sticking. Sometimes when broiling oily fish over coals, grease will drip down and cause flames to flare up. If this happens, briefly remove the grill holding the fish and flick water droplets on the flames to douse them.

Going back to Jimmy Bartok and our shoreline lake trout dinner, the method he used is actually quite well known among woodsmen, and is formally dubbed "plank broiling." Almost any clean plank of lumber is suitable, provided it is not from any of the coniferous tree species, as they will bleed pitch and resin that taint the flavor of the fish. It's a good idea to "season" the wood before using it for plank broiling. Do this by soaking the wood in cold water for 15 minutes and then liberally wiping it with cooking oil. The fish will remain intact better if the skin is left on. You can use common nails, if you prefer, instead of pegs to secure the slab of meat to the board.

Plank broiling is one of the few methods of outdoor cooking in which it is perfectly acceptable to have a robust fire rather than coals. Since the fish is positioned off to the side, the meat is not directly touched by the flames. If any breeze is blowing, position the plank upwind of the fire so the meat will receive no smoke or drifting soot particles.

Boiled Fish

It doesn't have a very fancy name but boiled fish is an elegant way to prepare almost any species, especially the white-fleshed, non-oily types such as pike and bass.

Poor Man's Lobster
2 pounds fish fillets
4 potatoes, peeled and quartered
2 onions, sliced
¼ cup evaporated milk
1 teaspoon flour
¼ teaspoon salt
¼ teaspoon black pepper
cold water

In a deep skillet place the potatoes, onion slices, salt and pepper, then add cold water until the above ingredients are just barely covered. Cover the skillet with a lid and simmer on low heat until the potatoes are half-done (about 15 minutes). Now lay the fish fillets on top of the potatoes and continue simmering until both the fish and potatoes are done. Very carefully remove the fish and place them on a plate in your oven where they will stay warm. Scald the evaporated milk and blend in the teaspoon of flour. Stir this into the potatoes and other ingredients and let everything bubble for a few minutes until a rich gravy has formed. Pour the works over the fish fillets and serve. Serves four.

Not many anglers are aware of it, but most fish species are very good when boiled, chilled, and later served cold. Here is a favorite around our place. Heat a kettle of lightly salted water to boiling. Drop into the water six to eight white-fleshed fish fillets, cover the pot and let the fish cook for two minutes...no longer! Remove the fish from the water, wrap in foil and place in your refrigerator overnight. The next day, shred the chilled meat with a fork and mix it into a robust chef's salad. When bass or pike are served this way, you probably won't be able to tell the difference between it and fresh crab or lobster!

Poached Fish

By definition, "poaching" means to simmer meat slowly while it is completely submerged in liquid. However, unlike boiling fish as previously described, poaching generally (but not always) is accomplished inside an oven, using a poacher or pan specially designed for the purpose. If you don't have such a device and don't want to spring for the

Poaching is another method well suited to large fish that are rough-dressed. The recommended liquid is a court bouillon, but do not let it boil. A slow simmer is best to achieve tender perfection as the vegetables and spices impart a very subtle hint of flavor.

price (quality copper poachers can wreak havoc with one's wallet), it's easy to substitute any type of deep frypan, kettle or large glass casserole dish.

Trout and salmon species are most commonly poached but virtually any fresh-water or salt-water species turn out fine, although the most desirable approach is to use whole fish, rough-dressed fish or thick fillet slabs, as opposed to small panfish.

The most widely used liquid for poaching fish is a court bouillon, made as follows:

Court Bouillon
3 cups water
1 small onion, sliced
¼ cup white vinegar
½ teaspoon salt
½ teaspoon black pepper
1 bay leaf
¼ teaspoon thyme

Add all the ingredients to a saucepan, bring the mixture to a boil, quickly reduce the heat, cover the pan and slowly simmer for 20 minutes. (There are many variations of court bouillon, most all of them ranging from good to excellent. For variety, try adding thinly sliced carrots, either celery slices or bits of parsley, and in the case of special dinners, 1 cup of white wine.) Keep in mind it may be necessary to proportionately vary the quantities of the above ingredients, depending upon how many diners you plan to serve and therefore how much fish you'll be cooking. The only rule of thumb is to have ample liquid to entirely cover the fish to be poached.

Your oven should be pre-heated to 425 degrees. Lightly grease the rack in your poacher, or smear a thin coating of margarine on the inside surfaces of your kettle or glass casserole dish. Place the utensil in the oven for a few minutes until it becomes very hot (not scorched!). With a potholder, remove the poacher or casserole dish, add one cup of steaming hot court bouillon, arrange your fish in the bottom of the vessel, then cover with the remaining liquid. Cover the poacher, return it to the oven, and let the fish slowly bubble in the cauldron until it flakes easily, about 10 minutes per inch of thickness of the fish.

To serve, remove individual pieces of fish with a large spatula.

This may take some careful juggling in the cases of large, whole fish since they will be very tender and care must be exercised to ensure that they do not fall apart. Place the fish on a hot serving platter and ladle over the top several tablespoons of the bouillon (use a slotted spoon to remove the vegetable pieces first).

Stews and Chowders

As the season draws to a close, anglers frequently begin cleaning out their freezers, making room for small game, upland birds, ducks and geese, and venison. The question is what to do with any remaining fish? Perhaps there is a pint-sized bass, a big ol' catfish, maybe a couple of bluegills, and a few other finny odds and ends, none of which individually is enough to make a meal.

Why not make a chowder? A chowder is ideally suited to using up miscellaneous pieces of fish, it takes almost no time at all, and you can throw into the pot any random ingredients that are merely taking up room in your pantry. If there is any chowder left, which is not likely, it can be frozen and reserved for some cold winter night in coming months when the closest thing to fishing are the nighttime dreams of lunkers. Best of all, chowders are one of the most delicious ways to prepare fish.

Fish Chowder

2 pounds fish, cut in ½-inch cubes
8 strips bacon
2 large onions, minced
4 potatoes, diced
½ cup evaporated milk
1 can condensed, creamed soup
3 cups water
1 teaspoon salt
½ teaspoon black pepper
1 teaspoon blended herbs

Slice the bacon into ½-inch squares and fry it in a skillet until crisp. When the bacon is done, remove it from the pan and set it aside on a paper towel to drain. In the bacon grease remaining in the pan, sauté the onions until they are clear. Transfer the bacon grease and onions to a large pot and add the fish, potatoes, water, herbs and spices. Cover the pot and let all of the ingredients simmer on low heat until the potatoes and fish are tender (about one hour). Stir in one can of condensed, creamed soup such as cream of mushroom, cream of celery, or cream of barley, and add ½ cup evaporated milk. Simmer the chowder until it is piping hot, but do not allow it to come to a boil. Serve in deep bowls with the bacon bits sprinkled on top. Serves four.

To vary this basic chowder recipe, try adding a diced green pepper, diced carrots or celery, or almost any other vegetable. Some even go as far as to add several cans of tomato sauce, but I look upon this as heresy.

I'm also very fond of catfish stew. Although it can be prepared at home, it's a special treat when served about midnight around a flickering shoreline fire while intermittently tending a trotline.

Catfish Stew
6 1-pound catfish
4 cups milk
4 cups water
4 potatoes, sliced
1 onion, chopped
2 celery stalks, chopped
3 tablespoons butter
½ teaspoon salt

Skin and rough dress the catfish and then boil them in a pot of lightly salted water for five minutes. Pour off the water, separate the meat from the bones and cut it into chunks. Place the meat back in the pot and add the remaining ingredients. Slowly simmer for one hour but do not allow it to boil, then serve piping hot. Serves four.

Side Dishes

Virtually all side dishes go well with fish. But with deepfried fish, hushpuppies seem to be a favorite with most anglers. (Deepfrying is almost exactly the same as panfrying except that more cooking oil is used and the fish are suspended in the cauldron in a wire basket.) The best-tasting hushpuppies are cooked in the same oil used to deepfry the fish (keep the fish warm in your oven while making the 'puppies), but fresh cooking oil also is suitable if the fish have been broiled, baked or prepared some other way in which liberal quantities of oil are not used.

Hushpuppies
3 cups yellow cornmeal
3 cups white flour
2 cups minced onion
5 eggs
1 tablespoon salt
6 teaspoons baking powder
6 teaspoons sugar
buttermilk

Combine all the ingredients in a large bowl, then slowly add just enough buttermilk to make a very thick batter. Then, holding the bowl over the pot of cooking oil, use a tablespoon to spoon off 1½-inch diameter globs of the batter. When the hushpuppies hit the hot oil they will momentarily sink to the bottom but they quickly swell up and float to the surface. Let them bubble away until they are dark golden brown on the outside and light and fluffy inside, then drain on absorbent toweling before serving.

Another dish that goes well with any fish dinner, and also combination fish-and-game dinners, is "timbales."

Timbales
1 cup cooked, flaked fish
2 cups cooked Minute Rice
2 eggs
⅛ teaspoon marjoram
¼ teaspoon salt
¼ teaspoon black pepper
cooking oil

Boil the fish (bass, striper, walleye or pike fillets equaling one pound in weight) in lightly salted water for four minutes, then remove and let cool slightly. Next, flake and shred the meat with a fork. In a bowl, mix the fish thoroughly with the other ingredients, then drop large spoonfuls of the timbales onto a sizzling hot griddle smeared with cooking oil and fry just like pancakes until golden brown. Serves four.

Going back to Bill Gressard, another superb accompaniment to any meal, even wild-game dinners, is his panfish cocktail. This recipe uses the same bluegill or sunfish fillets described earlier and the end result is almost identical to shrimp cocktail.

Simply place two pounds of fillets into a double-boiler or clam steamer and steam them until the flesh is firm (usually no longer than one minute). Chill overnight in your refrigerator, then serve with your favorite red cocktail sauce.

More Fish Recipes

At this point we should mention that there is wide room for flexibility in most fish recipes and in many cases an enterprising angler is limited only by his own ingenuity and personal tastes. Of course, if a poaching recipe states that fish should be simmered in a court bouillon for 10 minutes, you'll not want to extend the cooking time to 25 minutes, nor will you want to add three tablespoons of salt to a recipe calling for only ½ teaspoon. But with sound judgment, anglers should feel free to experiment occasionally by adding or substituting ingredients other than those a recipe may specifically call for.

Also realize that a great many recipes state that a particular species should be used, yet substitutions of entirely different species are often not only possible, but sometimes even joyously discovered to offer superior results. A bass recipe you like, for example, is almost certain to taste just as well, if not better, when followed accordingly but with walleyes or northern pike. The same philosophy applies with regard to the substitution of many salt-water species in recipes otherwise calling for a certain fresh-water species. The main thing to remember is to make substitutions only among fish of similar oil content. In other words, try using smallmouth bass in a recipe calling for striper, but don't try chinook salmon.

Ray Grob's Creamed Striper

2 pounds striped bass fillets
1 can condensed cream of mushroom soup
1 tablespoon milk

Add the condensed soup and milk to a saucepan over low heat and stir until smooth and hot. Meanwhile, lay the fish fillets in a buttered baking dish. Pour soup/sauce over the fillets and bake in an oven pre-heated to 350 degrees for 35 minutes. Serves four.

Broiled Rockfish with Bacon

4 1-pound striped bass steaks
4 strips thick bacon
salt and pepper

Very lightly salt and pepper the fish steaks, then wrap each with a strip of bacon held in place with a toothpick. Broil five to eight minutes per side. Serves four.

Mediterranean Striper

2 pounds striped bass steaks or thick fillets
1 tablespoon lemon juice
½ cup white wine
1 small onion, sliced
1 16-ounce can tomatoes, drained
1 clove garlic
1 teaspoon parsley flakes
1 teaspoon dried oregano
salt and pepper

Mix together all the ingredients except the fish and then run them through your food blender just until the tomatoes are coarsely chopped (no more than 10 seconds). Pour the sauce into a deep glass baking dish and place it in your oven, pre-heated to 450 degrees. When the sauce begins to bubble, lay the fish in the dish and spoon some of the sauce over the tops of them. Bake, uncovered, for 15 minutes or until the fish flakes easily, while frequently basting with more sauce. Gently remove fish to a hot serving platter and ladle several spoonfuls of the sauce over the fish. Serves four.

Dixieland Catfish

6 skinned, rough-dressed, 1-pound catfish
½ cup French dressing
1 lemon
paprika

Liberally brush the inside of each fish with the French dressing. Place two very thin lemon slices inside each body cavity and lay the catfish in a well-greased baking dish. Brush the outside of each fish with more French dressing, place another lemon slice on top of each fish and sprinkle with paprika. Bake in an oven pre-heated to 350 degrees for 30 minutes. Serves four.

New Orleans Delight

6 skinned, rough-dressed, 1-pound catfish
½ cup tomato sauce
2 packets ¾-ounce dry cheese-garlic salad dressing mix
2 tablespoons cooking oil
2 tablespoons parsley flakes
grated Parmesan cheese

Combine all ingredients except the Parmesan cheese to make a sauce and then liberally brush each fish inside and out. Lay the fish in a well-greased baking dish and sprinkle with the Parmesan cheese. Let stand for ½ hour, then bake in an oven pre-heated to 350 degrees for 30 minutes. When the fish are done, slide the baking dish under the broiler and lightly brown the tops of the fish (about three minutes) until they are barely crisp around the edges.

Plantation Catfish

6 rough-dressed, 1-pound catfish
1 cup flour
½ cup yellow cornmeal
12 slices bacon
2 teaspoons paprika
½ cup evaporated milk
1 tablespoon salt
½ teaspoon pepper

Fry the bacon in a cast-iron skillet until well done and then set aside where it will stay warm. Mix the milk, salt and pepper in one bowl. In another bowl mix the flour, cornmeal and paprika. Dip the fish in the milk mixture, shake off the excess, and roll in the flour mixture. Next, fry the catfish in the remaining bacon drippings for five minutes on one side, gently flip them over, then fry five minutes on the other side. Serve the fish on top of the bacon slices. Serves four.

Trout Almondine
6 rough-dressed, 1-pound trout
1 cup butter
½ cup slivered almonds
⅓ cup dry vermouth
1 tablespoon parsley flakes
½ cup flour
¼ teaspoon salt
¼ teaspoon black pepper

Add the flour, salt and pepper to a paper bag. Melt the butter in a frypan (to prevent clarifying, add one tablespoon cooking oil). Shake the trout in the paper bag until they are well dusted with flour, then fry over moderate heat for five minutes on each side. Remove the fish to where they will stay warm while browning the almonds in the butter. Stir in the vermouth and parsley flakes and simmer slowly until hot, then pour over the trout and serve. Serves four.

Baked Trout in Wine
2 pounds trout or salmon fillets
1¼ cup white flour
1 cup milk
1 cup butter
3 tablespoons white wine
¼ teaspoon tarragon

Smear the inside surfaces of a glass baking dish with the butter, then pre-heat your oven to 350 degrees. Add the tarragon to the flour, dip the fish fillets in the milk, coat with the flour, and place in the bottom of the baking dish. To the remaining butter, knead in the remaining flour to create a paste and spread this over the tops of the

Troute Meuniere being prepared by Bill Weiss on frozen Dow Lake in southern Ohio.
It is a simple recipe that deserves gourmet rating.

fish with a knife. Cover the dish and bake the trout for 20 minutes. Then sprinkle the white wine over the fish and continue baking uncovered until the fish have a golden brown crust. Serves four.

Trout Meuniere

4 rough-dressed, 1-pound trout
¼ pound sweet (unsalted) butter
½ cup flour
peanut oil
1 lemon, sliced in thin wedges
1 teaspoon salt
½ teaspoon pepper

Heat the butter in a skillet until the milk solids settle to the bottom, then spoon off the surface liquid. Add the salt, pepper and flour to a paper bag. Rinse the trout with cold water and shake off the excess, then add the trout one at a time to the paper bag and shake until the fish are well dusted. Fry the trout in the hot peanut oil for 5 or 6 minutes on each side until crispy brown. Reheat the butter until it turns amber in color (don't let it burn!). Transfer the trout to a preheated serving dish, pour the hot butter over the fish and serve with the lemon wedges. Serves four.

Cheesey Fish Casserole

2 pounds fish fillets (non-oily species)
1½ cups grated cheddar cheese
1 egg
1 cup milk
cracker meal (or breadcrumbs)
butter
½ teaspoon salt
¼ teaspoon pepper

Pre-heat your oven to 400 degrees. In a bowl, mix the egg and milk, then stir in the salt and pepper. Dip the fillets in the egg-milk mix, then roll in cracker meal or breadcrumbs. Lay the fish in the bottom of a well-buttered glass casserole dish and sprinkle the cheese over the top. Bake about 20 minutes or until the fish flakes easily. Serves four.

Butter-Herb Baked Fish
2 pounds fish fillets (non-oily species)
1 cup sweet (unsalted) butter
1½ cups crushed saltine crackers
½ cup grated Parmesan cheese
1 teaspoon basil leaves
1 teaspoon oregano leaves
½ teaspoon garlic powder
½ teaspoon salt

In a large baking dish melt the butter in an oven pre-heated to 350 degrees (about six minutes). Mix together the cracker crumbs, Parmesan cheese, basil, oregano, salt and garlic powder. Dip the fish fillets in the melted butter, then roll them in the seasoned crumb mixture. Arrange the fish fillets in the bottom of the baking dish and bake for 30 minutes or until the fish flakes easily. Serves four.

4

Field Care of Deer and Other Big Game

There is perhaps no other aspect of the outdoors more riddled with myths and misconceptions than the proper field care of big-game animals. Share a deer-hunting camp with even the most respectable, best-intentioned pals and one is nevertheless likely to see in use a variety of practices ranging from absurd to laughable.

You'll see many deer split wide open, from "stem to stern." Other hunters, when their deer is down, immediately run up and plunge their knife blade deep into the deer's throat because they believe it is necessary to bleed the animal. Many others stalwartly maintain that using water to clean out the chest cavity will ruin the meat. Tens of thousands of deer hunters every year literally do hatchet jobs on the deer's pelvic area, using axes and saws and leaving behind the amateur-ish appearance of damaged meat and jagged remnants of splintered bone. Some almost amputate the hind quarters in their misguided haste to remove the musk glands. I've even seen otherwise honorable hunters put their deer in their car trunks in the sweltering heat, slam the lid tight and let their venison broil during the long drive home.

Such butchered-up, botched-up deer do not say much on behalf of the hunters who took them because they represent a lack of knowledge of the proper care and treatment of animal carcasses. Many such deer, to be honest, end up tasting absolutely awful, which is regrettable because venison that has been cared for properly is far superior to many types of livestock meat, both in flavor and nutritional value.

So if you ever hear anyone complain of his or her dislike for venison because "it is too tough," or "it is too gamey tasting," or for some other reason, you can bet the grocery money there was some person involved in either the field dressing of the animal, the butchering or storage, or the actual meal preparation who had absolutely no idea of what he was doing and therefore resorted to guesswork or fable.

In this chapter we'll be looking at the right way to field-dress small to medium big-game animals such as whitetails, mule deer, blacktails and antelope. Then we'll examine the slightly different techniques that apply to larger big-game animals such as elk, moose and caribou. We'll also say a few words about bears. But before we begin, let's clear the air about a few fallacies that have existed for many, many years.

First, it's never necessary for a deer hunter, when his trophy is down, to remove its tarsal glands. These appear as slightly moist or sticky, dark tufts of hair surrounding inch-long gland slits located just below the knee on each rear hock. When a deer dies, the glands no longer function. And since they are located so far from the main body area, there is no way for them to touch or adversely affect the meat if you merely leave them alone. There was one time that I tasted venison that had been tainted by musk-gland scent, but this happened when a young boy in our camp took his first buck, and in his exuberance began needlessly cutting at the glands (at the advice of his father). He did a horrendously sloppy job and then, without washing his hands or the knife he was using, began handling the meat, allowing some of the gland's oil to be transferred. Good advice is simply to exercise a bit of caution *not* to touch or disturb the glands, and you'll have absolutely no trouble with them.

Neither do I see any reason whatsoever for cutting into a deer's neck region in a misguided belief that the animal must be bled. If the hunter has scored a good shot in a vital region, using a slug-loaded shotgun, centerfire rifle, muzzleloader or bowhunting equipment, the animal will have automatically bled itself and 98 percent of its blood will have drained into the chest cavity. You'll notice this for sure when you open the animal and the stuff pours out. Besides, after you've calmed down from the excitement of bagging your trophy and thought the matter through, you may decide to have the head mounted. There will be no chance of a taxidermist doing a satisfactory job if you've already ruined the neck skin.

It *is* imperative that the deer or other big-game animal be field-dressed as soon as possible, to reduce the temperature of all those steaks and roasts. From the time the animal dies until the time it eventually is reduced to wrapped packages for the freezer, keeping the meat cool is the number one concern.

But let's back up for just a moment. Well before you've centered your sights on your trophy, advance planning will save time and make everything go smoothly. Even before the hunt has begun, consider what you will have to do later when your deer or other big-game animal is down. Then, assemble the necessary equipment and buy whatever supplies you anticipate you'll need.

To dress a deer or pronghorn properly and then remove it from the field, only three items are needed. One is a sharp knife, preferably with a drop-point blade no more than four inches in length. You will also need some type of plastic bag for the animal's liver and heart; I like an old bread wrapper, for reasons I'll explain later. Last, obtain a hank of rope. Twenty feet of ¼-inch nylon rope with a tensile strength of 500 pounds should be more than sufficient.

In the cases of larger game animals such as elk and moose, the same type of knife is recommended but you may also find good use for some type of lightweight, folding belt saw. Due to the larger sizes of the heart and liver you'll need three bread wrappers. Some type of block and tackle or other mechanical hoist may prove invaluable (you needn't carry this while hunting; it can be left in your vehicle or back in camp). You'll need an assortment of muslin game bags made for the purpose of storing meat, and some type of packboard or backpack frame. Finally, you should have on hand two types of rope, one similar to that described above and a second hank of approximately ⅜- or ½-inch nylon that is at least 30 feet in length and has a tensile strength of at least 1500 pounds.

Lastly, at home or in camp prepare a place to hang your whole deer carcass, muslin meat bags, or elk or moose quarters. It may be from a tree, from the stout rafters in your garage, or in an open-air equipment shed. Just be sure that the place remains shaded for the better part of the day, that the hanging mechanism is strong enough to suspend a heavy load several feet off the ground, and that there is no danger of dogs, birds or other animals sampling your rewards.

Deer

Field-dressing a big-game animal need not be as complicated as many hunters make it. Basically, the procedure amounts to little more than rolling a deer over onto his back, opening the belly, allowing the warm

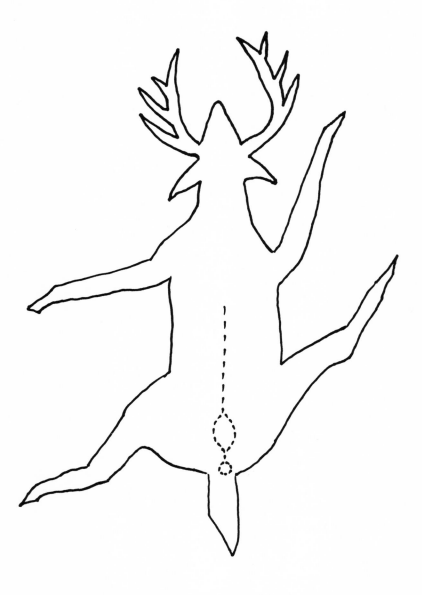

To field-dress deer or antelope properly, these are the only incisions required.

blood in the cavity to drain away, and removing the abdominal and chest organs.

If possible, position the deer with its head and shoulders slightly uphill or on higher ground. This will allow the blood and offal, when the deer is opened, to spill out and flow downhill and away from the carcass and your working area.

The best way to begin is by straddling your deer, facing the chest region. The job is a lot easier if a partner is available to hold either the front or rear legs upright, to prevent the deer from rolling over on its side. Some hunters working alone remedy the problem by straddling their deer in a kneeling position, holding the deer carcass upright and in place by exerting pressure with the insides of their knees. You can also brace the side of the deer against a log or rock.

To open the deer, grab the belly skin firmly between the thumb and forefinger, lift the skin up, and very carefully with just the tip of your knife blade slice a 1½-inch cut in the skin. The reason for lifting the skin up is so the knife blade, if it happens to go just a little too deep, has no chance of cutting into the intestines lying directly beneath.

Now, slip two fingers (the index and middle fingers, palm facing up) into the hole you've just created, spread your fingers slightly and lift, then carefully place the tip of your knife between your fingers with the blade edge facing up. While lifting up the abdominal skin, guide the blade down the centerline of the animal from the reproductive organs to the base of the rib cage. The intestines and paunch will now bulge up and begin to spill out. Be careful not to touch them with your knife blade or you'll soon have messy digestive matter everywhere.

Now, using mostly your hands, begin gently pulling the remainder of the paunch and viscera out of the abdominal cavity. These should come away rather freely and you will eventually come upon the diaphragm, a skin-like wall that separates the abdomen from the upper chest region. Carefully cut this away from its attachment surrounding the rib cage, plus any other small restraining ligaments still holding onto the abdominal organs.

With the offal lying on the ground beside the deer, yet still connected to the reproductive area, the next order of business is removing the heart and lungs. In doing this, there is no need to borrow a double-bit lumberjack axe and begin chopping away at the rib cage, as I have actually seen a few hunters do.

Simply roll up your sleeves, kneel, and with your knife in one

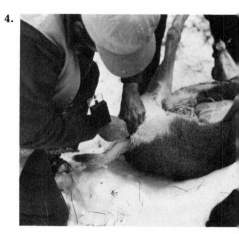

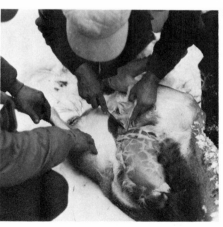

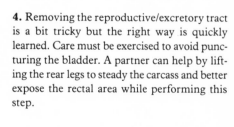

1. Lay the deer on its back with its head slightly uphill. Pinch the abdominal skin, lift, and make a small cut just large enough for your fingers. Then guide the knife blade carefully to the base of the sternum, no farther.

2. After removing the paunch and organs higher up in the chest cavity, turn around and face the other end of the animal and lengthen the abdominal cut to go around the reproductive organs.

3. Care must be exercised to ensure you do not cut into the prime rump roasts when cutting around the reproductive organs.

4. Removing the reproductive/excretory tract is a bit tricky but the right way is quickly learned. Care must be exercised to avoid puncturing the bladder. A partner can help by lifting the rear legs to steady the carcass and better expose the rectal area while performing this step.

hand extend both arms as far as you can reach up through the chest cavity and into the neck region, and grab the esophagus and windpipe. These will feel, in your hands, like two tubes lying one on top of the other: a ¾-inch diameter soft one, and a 1½-inch diameter ribbed one.

Completely sever this twin-tube assembly as high up as you can reach and then withdraw the hand holding the knife. With the other hand get a firm hold on the esophagus/windpipe tubes and begin pulling backwards, and along with the tubes the heart and lungs also will come back and out just like a banana being peeled. At this time you can trim away tissue surrounding and/or connected to the heart, and also the liver which now is exposed, and set them on a clean rock or bed of moss or ferns to drain.

The next step is completing the removal of the intestines and the reproductive/excretory tract. Again, don't go fetch a hatchet and start chopping away at the aitch-bone or pelvis or anything else. Many hunters do this, and nine times in ten they puncture the bladder, rupture the colon so that fecal matter spills out or in some other manner damage the precious, inner hindquarter meat.

Initially, we made a cut into the abdomen and worked upwards toward the chest region. Now we want to reverse our line of travel and work in the opposite direction toward the reproductive/excretory tract. So turn around and face the hindquarters, still straddling the deer. If the abdominal slice has not gone all the way to the base of the penis, lengthen that cut at this time.

Next, grab the penis itself and lift it gently while carefully cutting around both sides; since it lies on top of the skin, the cut does not have to be deep. Still holding the penis, extend the cut in a narrow Y-fashion to go along both sides of the testicles. As you are doing this, the organ should begin lifting away; but, to repeat, make sure your knife goes no deeper than ⅛ inch deep because immediately beneath the thin skin in this region lies the hindquarter meat. Should the animal happen to be a doe (or cow, as in the case of elk, moose or caribou), the procedure just outlined is basically the same except the cuts around the testicles instead go around the vagina.

As the two cuts pass on either side of the testicles (or vagina) and approach the region of the anus they will briefly come slightly together again, but then quickly will have to be widened again to go all the way around the anal opening. Once this circular cut has been made, the anal opening will appear to have a small edge or flap of skin all the way around the diameter of the orifice. Grab this skin with your finger-tips and then with the very tip of your knife blade begin very gently cutting and separating the anal tube from the inside of the pelvic canal. This is where a partner really comes in handy because he can grab the hind legs and lift, better exposing the anal region. If no partner is available, one trick is to stand facing away from the deer but backed up against it with the animal's hind legs *behind* your thighs, and the side of the animal braced against a log or rock. As you back up just a step more, the anal region is both raised and exposed, so that bending at the waist will give you easy access to it.

"Reaming out the bunghole," as it is commonly called, sees the circular cut made to a depth of about 4½ inches; the deeper you go into the pelvic canal, the more care must be exercised not to slice into the bladder. Here is one advantage of the four-inch knife blade, as it will not allow you to penetrate too deeply, perchance pierce the bladder, and suddenly have a flood of urine gushing all over. In fact, as added insurance that this does not happen, once you've reamed the canal to a depth of about three inches, it's usually best to stop working from this direction and begin coming in from the other end (the abdominal side).

Grab the lower intestine, pull it back slightly and, gently working around the bladder, begin the same circular cutting-and-separating motion down through the pelvis. Soon, cuts made from this direction will meet those from the other side, or nearly so, and you'll be able to pull out the entire reproductive and excretory tract intact and undamaged.

The procedure described here may sound complicated. But when you become proficient at it, as are hunters who take a deer or other big-game animal almost every year, the entire job of field-dressing an animal should take no more than 10 or 12 minutes.

The deer's insides should now be entirely cleaned out and you should be noticing steam rising from the carcass, a happy sight indicating the meat is beginning to cool. I like now to roll the carcass over on its belly, with its legs spread wide, so that the open body cavity has a few minutes more to drain any blood or body fluids still trapped inside. During this time I work on the heart and liver, which now themselves should be fully drained, trimming as necessary to remove unwanted tissue or restraining ligaments still attached to the organs. Then I place them in my plastic bag or bread wrapper.

When the deer carcass is fully drained, roll the animal onto its back again and use several handfuls of clean leaves, moss, snow or dry grass to wipe the inside of the body cavity clean of any remaining debris. It's not necessary to spend a great deal of time in this because (as described later) you'll be doing a more thorough clean-up job when you arrive home or in camp.

The last order of business is securing the plastic bag containing the heart and liver *inside* the animal's chest cavity. This is why I like to use a long, narrow bread wrapper. Twist the long tail of the bread wrapper and from the inside of the chest cavity push the end of the tail out through a small knife cut made between two of the ribs (or through the bullet hole). Then, tie a large knot in the tail of the bread wrapper, so that the knot is snug against the outside of the hide. This nifty little trick keeps the liver/heart bag firmly secured inside the body cavity of the animal, which is much better than trying to cram the irregularly shaped, eight-pound glob of meat in one of your coat pockets.

Your deer is now completely field-dressed and ready to be removed to camp or a waiting vehicle. Even in this, there are right ways, and wrong ways that cause nothing but hardship and sometimes even meat spoilage. We'll cover the subject thoroughly in the next chapter. Meanwhile, let's examine the procedure for field-dressing larger game animals such as elk and moose.

Elk and Other Larger Game Animals

In the vast majority of cases whitetails, mule deer, antelope and similar big-game animals are only roughly field-dressed at the kill site and then transported to camp or home where they are subsequently skinned and butchered. The only exception to this is in rare situations when such an animal is killed in exceedingly rugged terrain and the only physical way to remove it to camp is in pieces, sometimes known as "quarters."

Just the opposite applies to the largest North American game animals such as elk, moose and caribou. Almost never are these animals transported whole to camp or home as their enormous body weights prohibit such handling. Instead, they are not only field-dressed at the kill site but also skinned and cut up into easily handled pieces.

Field-dressing such animals – removing warm blood, viscera and internal organs – is accomplished in fundamentally the same manner that was previously described for deer. There are a few minor exceptions, but basically you're simply working with a much larger animal that is almost identical in body conformation. Therefore the field-dressing operation merely takes more time and requires considerably more muscle power.

As with deer, the best way to field-dress an elk, moose or caribou is with the animal lying on its back. In manhandling the carcass about, the long legs often can be used to good advantage, or a lever and fulcrum can be contrived from a stout pole and either a rock or short log. In any event, this is merely to adjust the position of the animal and make it more convenient to work on it – I shudder at the back-breaking thought of even attempting to move such giant animals more than a few feet from where they have fallen.

Instead of making one long knife cut through the centerline of the animal's abdomen, as with deer, many hunters like to remove an oval-shaped piece of abdominal skin. This skin will be about a foot wide and run from the base of the rib cage all the way back past the reproductive organs (which come away easily with the hide) to the anus. The reason for removing this hide is that the hair in this region typically is thick and matted with foul urine, excrement, wallow mud and other lip-curling goo that is not at all pleasant to work around and will taint any meat it comes in contact with. After this patch of hide is removed and discarded, thoroughly clean your knife and hands with snow or damp moss before proceeding with other dressing chores in the standard manner.

Once the elk or moose is field-dressed, and still lying on its back, prop open the body cavity with sticks to allow heat to escape. To ensure the animal remains on its back and doesn't flop over, it's a good idea to brace the carcass with logs, rocks or whatever is available.

Generally, depending upon the circumstances, the next step is to return to camp for other equipment that will be needed. To ensure your carcass is not bothered in your absence by bears, coyotes, birds or other scavengers, it is wise to cover it loosely with pine boughs gathered from a still-green blowdown. These branches will still allow ample air circulation around the animal's body but discourage assorted critters from investigating. I further place an article of my clothing on top of the bough-covered carcass as the strong odor of man-scent usually will keep all but the most desperate creatures at bay. The best item to use is your T-shirt which, after the day's hunt and the field-dressing chores, should be quite odoriferous.

In hiking back to camp, take the animal's liver and heart with you. These will weigh quite a bit and may be about all you'll be able to comfortably handle (remember, you'll also have in your possession your rifle, binoculars and other hunting equipment).

Upon arriving in camp, place the liver and heart in a pan of salted water to soak out any blood still remaining in the organs. Then, exchange your hunting gear for your backpack frame, mechanical hoist, folding belt saw, rope and muslin game bags, and return to the kill site. (If the daily air temperature is below 50 degrees, and the night temperature much cooler, you can wait until the following day to return to your animal. However, if the temperature is much higher than this, it's imperative to return as quickly as possible and even work by lantern light if necessary, due to the insulating properties of the thick hides such large animals possess.)

At this point we should briefly mention equipment considerations. The same type of knife commonly used in dressing deer is also suitable for larger animals, but it's a good idea to have along some type of small whetstone for periodically touching up the blade. When purchasing meat bags, don't obtain those made of cheesecloth or other thin fabrics as they just don't have the strength to stand up to packing activities or the stress incurred when such bags are filled with meat and hung in trees during the interim. What you want are relatively thick muslin game bags made especially for the purpose (they can be washed and reused many times over the years).

The mechanical hoist I've mentioned several times also should be more thoroughly described. Forget about the little $4.95 "sportsmen's winches" you see in mail-order catalogs and sporting-goods stores, that have six-inch aluminum frameworks with small plastic pulleys inside and about 20 feet of thin rope. These sometimes are suitable for lifting deer and antelope off the ground, but all advertising claims to the contrary, they are not worth a hoot when it comes to handling creatures that may weigh in excess of 1,000 pounds. What you want is the type of comealong or ratchet winch sold in auto parts and farm supply stores, that has a heavy steel or cast-iron framework with a sturdy hook welded on top of the device, a spool filled with ¼- or ⅜-inch diameter woven wire cable with another hook on the end, and a heavy-duty cranking handle. Many varieties and designs are

The same type of knife used to field dress deer will suffice when handling larger game animals. But even better is a knife with a saw blade for necessary bone cutting.

available and the price will probably set you back a "C-note," but such a mechanical hoist will last a lifetime and in addition to handling big-game animals is sure to find many other uses during the year in conjunction with your boat or four-wheel-drive vehicle.

In skinning an elk or moose the method unanimously accepted as best is first to use just the tip of your knife blade to cut through the skin around the diameter of one of the hind legs, in the knee region, to expose the hock and Achilles' tendon. Then, depending upon how your particular ratchet winch works, place one hook through a cut made in the skin between the hock and Achilles tendon, somehow secure the other hook or cable over a stout tree branch or around a tree trunk (in either case at least 10 feet off the ground), and slowly begin lifting your animal.

Don't lift the carcass entirely off the ground just yet. Raise it just a little bit to a comfortable working level, begin removing the hide from the hind legs, then raise it a little more to tackle the rump and mid-body areas, then still a little more to skin the front shoulders and legs, and so on. As the animal is gradually lifted and skinned, the hide will drape down and out of the way. Continue this operation all the way down the neck to just below the animal's chin region, then cut the hide entirely free and set it aside. (This step assumes the hunter will be saving only the antlers and not having a full head mount. If a head mount is desired, you'll of course want to ensure the hide remains attached to the head and that the length of the remaining cape extends back several inches behind the front shoulder.)

Next, cut through the neck meat just below the ears until you reach the neck bone. Sometimes by grabbing the antlers and twisting you can break the neck bone and the head will fall free, but in most cases it's a lot easier if you use your folding saw for this operation.

With the fully skinned carcass now hanging, you can also use your saw to remove the two front lower legs just below the knees.

Next comes the business of further reducing the carcass to somewhat smaller meat portions that can later be carried back to camp on your back.

First, cut the neck meat from the carcass by running your knife down the back of the neck, on centerline, to the beginning of the front shoulders, then carefully removing it from around the diameter of the neck bone. Place this neck meat on the hide lying on the ground hair-side down, where it will stay clean. Or, if flies are a problem, secure the meat in one of the muslin game bags and hang it from a nearby tree branch.

Next, remove the two front shoulders and legs by easily running your knife beneath the flat scapula (shoulder blade). Again, place the meat on the hide or in game bags.

At this point you can begin reversing your earlier step of raising the carcass by lowering it in small increments to work on the back, hind legs and so on.

Some hunters like to cut out the backstraps; others prefer to leave them intact, saving the entire rib/backbone part of the anatomy in order to later saw horizontal, inch-thick steaks. It's really nothing more than personal preference, but, as I'll describe more fully in Chapter 6, I firmly believe in doing as little bone sawing as possible. I prefer to bone out the various cuts of meat, because boned cuts not only offer better eating on the dinner table but also take up less freezer space. Then too, since you can't eat bones, why go to all the trouble of carrying the heavy things out of the woodlands?

Removing the hind legs is also easily accomplished with no need to saw bones. With your knife blade make a deep cut that closely follows the backbone to the root of the tail, then make a similar cut on the inside of each hind leg. If you go slowly and carefully, the ball and socket eventually will be exposed, and you can easily slice right through the ligament that connects these two bones and free the leg from the carcass.

Next you'll want to go back over the carcass to trim away any other portions of meat still remaining along the backbone, front shoulders, rib cage, brisket and hindquarter region. The goal is to carry out as much pure meat and as little bone as possible (only that which remains inside the legs), and leave behind only the bare skeleton.

In the event that no tree is available for hanging your elk, moose or caribou there is no alternative but to skin the animal on the ground. It's quite an undertaking, but it can be done.

Field-dress the animal in the usual manner. Then, with the animal lying on its side, prop up one hind leg with a stout forked stick and begin carefully removing the hide. When the leg is entirely exposed, cut it free of the carcass in the same way as if the carcass were hanging. Then begin removing the hide from the lower chest and abdominal region, working progressively higher up the side of the body and folding the hide back as you go. Eventually, after you extend a shallow cut down the centerline of the rib cage to the chin, the front leg and shoulder will be exposed and can be duly removed. Then remove the backstraps and one side of the neck meat. Next remove all four lower legs, and the head and antlers, to reduce the total carcass weight as much as possible, so that you can roll the carcass over onto the skin-side of the hide you've just removed and repeat the procedure on the opposite side.

In skinning a larger game animal, removing legs and meat portions from the carcass can be a tiring job. It may be best to hang most of the meat to cool, pack out just one load during your return to camp, and wait until the following day to make additional trips for the other portions and also the hide and horns. However, each hunter will have to determine for himself which approach is best in accordance with existing weather conditions. If there is any choice in the matter, allow the meat to hang overnight at the kill site because when it is thoroughly chilled it becomes stiff and is much easier to handle. In this state the meat is also far less susceptible to bruising. Just remember, when leaving your big-game meat in the hinterland ensure that it is protected from birds, flies or scavengers. If you're in muskeg country or above timberline, and there are no trees for hanging your game bags, suspend them from a tripod of sticks lashed together at the apex, or set them upon rocks or whatever else may be available, to allow adequate circulation of air around and beneath the bags.

Goats, Sheep and Bears

Goats and sheep are field-dressed about the same as deer and other big-game animals. If a packhorse or mule is available, the trophy can be transported whole. But if the terrain is too rugged, take the meat, hide and head and leave the skeleton behind, cutting off the front and rear legs, neck meat and other portions in the same manner as when field-quartering an elk or moose.

Bears are field-dressed the same as deer, and since their body weights commonly run from 150 to 300 pounds, handling them is not as difficult a chore as it often is with some other big-game animals. In many cases, bears can be removed from the backcountry whole, by means of horseback or a four-wheel-drive machine. The thing to avoid is dragging such an animal across the ground as that would surely

ruin the hide. If no horse or four-by is available, it's necessary to skin the animal in the field, quarter it, then pack out the meat, hide and head.

Bears can be easily skinned the same as larger animals by first lifting them off the ground with some type of ratchet winch or block and tackle. Or, they can be skinned and dressed right on the ground in the same way as described for elk. The one exasperating thing about bears is that they typically have fat layers, particularly along the back, that unlike the tallow on hooved big-game animals are slick and greasy and annoying to handle.

There are two other things to consider. Most hunters like to have rugs made from their bear hides, so you will want to be very careful in your field-dressing and skinning operations not to damage the hide.

Extend the abdominal field-dressing cut on centerline to the base of the chin, and in the opposite direction to the root of the tail. From this centerline cut, make four additional cuts also running on centerline along the insides of the four legs to the base of the paws. When you reach the paws *don't* sever them free of the hide as they add to the attractiveness of the rug. Merely expose the lower leg bone at the base of the paw and cut through it with your folding saw so that the leg meat may be removed. In most cases it's wise to go no further and leave any additional skinning of the paws and head region to your taxidermist.

Bears can be field dressed on the ground, but it's much easier if the carcass can be hoisted from a tree limb. If the animal is taken during the spring season, the work is likely to be hot and greasy, due to the warm, humid weather and the tallow layers that bears acquire. *Photo by Bob Gilsvik*

5

Getting Big Game Home

Removing a deer or other big-game animal from the field to home or camp is just plain hard work (I call it a labor of love). But like anything else there are right ways and wrong ways, and some of the methods I've seen hunters use take the subject out of the category of work and transform it into an agonizing ordeal.

For example, you've seen magazine pictures of two guys carrying a deer that is trussed upside-down to a long pole they are supporting over their shoulders. The scene is exciting, outdoorsy, and makes the models look like macho woodsmen. But just try it! You'll continually stumble and fall off balance because of the bouncing, shifting carcass which is dead weight with a high center of gravity. By the time you get the animal out of the woods your neck will throb with pain and your entire shoulder will be rubbed raw. Whoever came up with this idea (don't blame the Indians; they had more practical outdoor savvy than the hype generated on Madison Avenue these days) deserves some kind of award, and I can think of nothing more fitting than bandages and liniment for their sore necks and shoulders.

Simply grabbing the antlers and heaving-ho is just about as un-wise, unless a partner is available to help and the drag is only for a very short distance. Since the dead-weight center of gravity now is very low to the ground (on the ground!), as is the head region, a lone hunter has to bend over to grab the horns and drag while continually hunched over. By the time you arrive at your vehicle, it will feel almost impossible to stand straight up again. Also, using this method, if you ever slip or stumble those sharp antler tines will go right into your calf muscles.

Perhaps the height of stupidity—and believe it or not, pictures of this method have even been allowed to appear in national sportsmen's magazines that claim to profess hunting safety—is using the so-called fireman's carry, whereby the deer is transported on top of the shoulders, around the neck, with the hunter holding the legs. They never say how you're supposed to get that floppy, awkward bulk of 175 pounds up on your shoulders in the first place, or how to clean the blood and body-oil stains out of your new down jacket, but those things are beside the point. Should the hunter stumble and fall, that enormous weight on top of him could prove fatal. It could break the hunter's back or snap his neck; or one of the deer's antler tines could go into his body like a spear. Just as important, traipsing through the woods with antlers, deer head, buckskin and flopping white tail hung about your neck is a dandy invitation to some irresponsible dolt to take a shot at you. It has happened!

There is only one right way to drag a deer, and amazingly it is the safest and involves the least amount of effort. First, extend the buck's front legs, lift up the hooves, and place each behind the animal's antlers so the front legs are up and out of the way, eliminating the resistance they would otherwise cause if allowed to drag on the ground. Now, loop your drag rope around the base of the antlers at the skull, perhaps taking a few additional turns around the hooves as well to prevent them from working loose, and tie a secure knot. Then look for a stick lying around. It should be sturdy, about 2 inches in diameter and about 25 inches long.

The other end of the drag rope should now be tied to the middle of the drag stick and then wrapped around as many more times as necessary so that the stick is eventually brought up to within about 2½ feet of the deer's head. With your hands behind your back, grab onto the stick; you can now begin relatively easily dragging out your deer. Further, you can stand at normal height while dragging to lessen fatigue or any chance of strained muscles. With a partner, each hunter grabbing onto one side of the stick, the job is even easier. In any case, gloves make pulling on the stick a lot more comfortable.

If it's an average-size buck, you'll have to stop to rest every so often. I suggest stopping every 50 yards, and here's why. In the past I've found that after my deer has been dragged out, I've had to make a second trip back to the kill site to retrieve my portable tree stand and other gear. I now eliminate the extra work by bringing my deer and hunting gear out in leap-frog fashion. This trick also eliminates having the extra weight of my rifle on my shoulder while dragging my deer. In other words, I drag my deer 50 yards, stop, go back 50 yards to pick up my stand, rifle, and other gear such as coat and binoculars, carry them 50 yards beyond my deer, and so on. This change of pace, I've found, makes dragging a deer far less tiring. Also, as I'm carrying forward my equipment, I have the opportunity to do a little scouting for the easiest drag route to take advantage of slight changes in the elevation of the terrain, because whenever possible you'll want to drag on the level or downhill. I also use this time to move aside any logs, rocks or other obstacles that may be blocking that route. When dragging, take a minute now and then to consider what type of terrain lies in the distance, so that you can alter your course of travel if need be

Dragging a deer with a short rope tied to the antlers and a stout stick is the easiest method for bringing an animal out of the hinterland. Here, Whitey Ellard (right) helps the author with a trophy mule deer taken in Colorado's White River National Forest.

If two relatively small deer are taken, they can both be dragged at once. Use the leap-frog method to plan the easiest route and remove obstacles from the trail. *Photo by Dave Richey*

to circumvent extremely dense cover or a stretch of jumbled landscape. I sometimes go out of my way, meaning a slightly longer dragging distance, if I'm able to find a long stretch of dry leaves, pine needles or very dry snow, because the carcass slides so much more easily on these.

One alternative to a drag rope is one of those shoulder harnesses you now see in sporting-goods stores. Generally, they consist of wide webbing material that buckles around your shoulders and waist, with a rope going off the backside that is tied to the deer's head. I once tested one of these by dragging a very heavy railroad tie around my back yard and I was amazed at how easy the job was with such a harness. I could go a hundred yards at a time without even having to stop and catch my breath. But then I later tried to drag a real buck and encountered the major problem of the antlers continually digging into the ground or getting snagged in trailside brush, which is something that doesn't often happen when using the drag technique I described earlier. I guess the best advice here, before buying such a harness, is to borrow one from a friend and see whether or not you like it.

One nifty tool for bringing out antelope, which is coming into very common use, is the "big wheel." The device looks somewhat like a wheelbarrow, except it has an old bicycle wheel instead of a small rubber tire, and instead of the deep metal bucket that a wheelbarrow has, it has a narrow support bed made from wooden slats. A big wheel can be made from scrap materials or those found in a salvage yard, and the only time involved is a free Saturday afternoon. Antelope are not heavy animals (field-dressed, averaging only 100 pounds) and getting them onto the big wheel framework requires only a simple trick. The big wheel is turned upside-down, laid on top of the pronghorn, which is thoroughly lashed in place with rope. Then, after grabbing the handles and bracing the wheel with your foot, you merely pull back and the thing pops right up. I suppose a big wheel could also be used when hunting whitetails and mule deer in hospitable terrain, but it works especially well for antelope due to the nature of their flat, plains-type habitat.

Backpacking and Horsepacking

Whitetails and antelope generally are taken relatively close to (within a mile of) some type of road or trail, and since such creatures typically are not so heavy, dragging is often the most practical method of removing them from the field.

However, it's an altogether different affair when dealing with mule deer, elk, moose, caribou, bears and some other species, which can be exceedingly heavy and more often than not meet their makers way back in the hinterland. In these situations a lucky hunter has three choices: pack the animal out on a horse's back, pack it out on his own back, or sit down and begin eating.

Play it smart and use any and all transportation to get a game animal to camp safely and quickly. Here, Dave Richey admires his trophy caribou as he relaxes in an inflatable raft carrying the load. *Photo by Kay Richey*

Horses (or mules) do a splendid job but many times add unexpected adventure to the outing because they do not at all like wild-game animals (particularly bears!) on their backs. In the annals of this country's hunting history, more than one dobbin has spooked and gone tearing off for home dragging hides, horns and meat bags behind him.

Just getting a whole mule deer up onto the back of a horse can be an adventure (and an exercise in frustration). First, tie the horse's reins to something and make sure he is calm. Then use something to blindfold him (a lightweight hunting jacket works as well as anything, with the sleeves tied behind the head). Then, and only then, drag the deer up next to the horse for the loading chore. Two men can use the Armstrong method of getting the deer up onto the horse's back, but if you're alone it's nearly impossible. In this case you'll have to position the horse next to a slightly elevated boulder or ledge, drag the deer a short distance and come in from the top. Better yet, hang the deer from a tree branch, move the horse in close, grab the lower legs of the deer, swing them over the horse's back and then slowly and gently let off on the rope so the forward end of the animal comes down on the opposite side of the horse. Make sure your ropes are secure!

I'm assuming here that either horses have been rented or you're hunting with an outfitter. Even if you aren't actually using horses during your daily hunting activities, it's wise, before the season opens, to contact a local rancher or two, just to find out who has horses available for hire if the need should arise. Maybe it will turn out that you'll be able to get your four-wheel-drive vehicle relatively close to the kill site, or perhaps you foresee no problems in packing the meat out on your back. But it's nice to know, if the animal is located in upside-down terrain, or if you happen to sprain your ankle, just where to go to obtain help in bringing out your animal.

Although horses and mules are occasionally used to bring out whole animals such as deer and bear, larger animals such as elk are customarily field-dressed, skinned and quartered; then bags of meat are brought out on the horse's back. Make sure the heavy game bags are equally distributed on both sides of the horse's back and that antler

Even if you're not using horses or mules for your hunting, contact a rancher in case help is needed. Here, Wilbur Luark helps Al and Mike Wolter bring a trophy muley out of a deep canyon, across the Colorado River and up a steep three-mile grade to camp.

In lashing meat and trophy antlers to packhorses, care must be taken to ensure that no sharp protrusions will gouge an animal's back or withers. *Photo courtesy of Gabby Barrus*

tines are not allowed to gouge the horse's hide. The trophy's hide should be protected as well because rubbing or chafing will inflict damage. Generally, the best method is to thoroughly salt the hide, then roll it up into a long cylinder shape that can conveniently be tied down some place.

Bringing out an animal piecemeal on your back is the next best bet. Any standard, lightweight backpack frame (with the pack bag removed) is suitable, and you'll need several six-foot lengths of lightweight rope to lash the load in place.

If the weather is cold and therefore insects are not presenting a problem, many hunters merely lash quarters, legs or other large chunks of meat (in bags) directly to their pack frames. But in general, it's wiser to make a number of trips carrying relatively light loads, rather than overburden yourself with too much meat and risk a fall or sprained ankle.

Take the best cuts of meat first – the hind legs, then the loins, and so on. For most hunters, 60 pounds should be the maximum weight they should try to carry. Remember, you've got a long way to go, and many trips to make, so take it slow and easy and rest often.

There is little difficulty in tying front legs, rear legs or rib sections to a pack frame. But other lumpy, soft items such as the neck meat, tenderloins, trimmings and the like, which have gone into cloth sacks, require special attention. Usually the best approach is to twist the neck of the bag and slip a noose of rope around it and tie this off near the top-center of the packframe. Then, with other ropes, criss-cross back and forth to secure the lower portions of the meat bag to the frame.

With any load you plan to carry, try to ensure that it is secured as

With big game such as elk and moose, removing animals whole to camp usually is impossible. They must be taken out in pieces, using backpack frames and cloth game sacks. Tip: Don't carry more than 70 pounds with each load, and stop to rest often.

high up on the packframe as possible without being tippy or top-heavy. Then, make sure the packframe's belt is snuggly cinched around your waist. This lets your hip region and upper back muscles do most of the work; they are far stronger and less susceptible to strain than your lower back, shoulder and arm muscles.

A word of caution: during the final one or two packing-out trips you'll be carrying the hide and antlers on your pack, and it is imperative that you take steps to ensure some other hunter does not see the horns and skin and mistake you for an animal. The best advice is to rummage around in your closet at home (before the trip) for an old fluorescent orange hunting vest that is beyond repair. Use scissors to cut the bright orange plastic into long strips or streamers, then later tie them to the antlers and hide on the back of your packframe. In fact, many hunters like to do this when using a horse or mule to bring out their trophy.

Camp Care of Game Meat

In a deer camp, whole deer traditionally are hung on a meatpole to keep the carcass cool and clean, and certainly so the game may be admired a while longer. Some hunters hang their deer by the antlers, others by the hind legs, all claiming it's mostly a matter of personal preference. I greatly disagree because there are several valid reasons why hanging a deer by the hind legs is far and away the better method.

First, body heat can escape from the carcass more easily when a deer is hung by the hind legs. When the carcass is hung by the antlers, body heat, which has a tendency to rise, is trapped in the chest, rib cage and neck cavity regions.

Another thing is that in the case of any animal such as a deer, the vast majority of the animal's blood and body fluids are located in the forward one-third of the body. Most of the blood has been removed during field-dressing operations but there may still be a bit in the body's smaller veins and arteries, and when an animal is hung it will begin to drain very slowly. The same is true with certain other fluids, but in any event you'll want these to exit as quickly as possible, not drain down slowly all over the carcass. You'll remember that during field-dressing operations the windpipe and esophagus tubes were severed high up in the neck region, so if the deer is hung by the hind

Hunters often debate how to hang their deer in camp. In northern Maine, these nice whitetails hang by the head. Note sticks placed in the abdominal wall to spread the opening to speed cooling.

legs any excess fluids that want to drain away will simply follow a natural course downhill and pass out through the nostrils and mouth without contacting any of your precious cuts of meat. In fact, a day or two later you'll notice a little puddle on the ground directly beneath the animal's head.

I like to use a big-game gambrel for hanging deer. Quality models cost less than $10 and can be ordered through mail-order houses that carry hunting equipment. They are also available in some sporting-goods stores. Another option is to purchase a gambrel from a farm supply dealer (get the size intended for butchering hogs, not the larger one used for beef steers). If you have a home workshop you can even make your own gambrel from pipe or reinforcing rod, with hooks welded on each end.

To use a gambrel, first make two small slices in the vicinity of each hock, through the thin skin that separates the leg bone from the Achilles tendon. Then merely insert the gambrel, tie a rope to the top-center, throw it over a tree limb or meatpole, and hoist the deer high enough so its head is about two feet off the ground. Now is when one of those miniature block and tackles comes in handy, as it allows a lone hunter to lift deer that may weigh as much as 250 pounds; otherwise you'll have to summon the help of a few friends and use the popular Armstrong method of lifting the deer.

Since leaves, mud and other debris are likely to have accumulated in the body cavity during the drag out, a more thorough cleaning of the carcass should now be undertaken.

Use your knife to trim away fat globules and remnants of torn or

Many hunters – the author included – favor hanging deer by the rear legs. This way, warm air won't rise and get trapped in the chest cavity.

bloodshot skin damaged by your bullet. If the weather is warm and these are allowed to remain on the carcass, they may encourage growth of spoilage organisms.

After this, I use a garden hose (turned on low-stream) or a pail of clean water to wash from the body cavity and neck region whatever blood residue may remain. I believe this is very important if the carcass is to hang and age for several days. The dirty water will drain all the way through, exiting from the nostrils, when the deer is hanging by its hind legs. The only thing to remember in any use of water is that it be used sparingly, that it not be allowed to directly contact bare meat — only the inside body walls of the carcass — and that it be permitted to air-dry very quickly, as any type of prolonged moisture will encourage the growth of bacteria. When the washing is completed, I may even go over the inside body cavity walls with a dry rag or handful of paper toweling to sop up any moisture left behind. All of these things result in a clean, presentable carcass that is far more pleasant to work with than one that is dirty and stained with dried blood.

You should now insert one or more sticks crosswise in the body cavity to spread the walls and speed cooling of the meat.

Hunters may wish to take other steps at this time, depending upon the weather. If it is typically cold at night but fairly warm during the day, hang the animal in the shade. That way, it will cool sufficiently during the night hours to remain cool through the warming afternoon the following day. If flies become a problem during these brief warm periods of the day, pull a cloth game bag over the deer. I like the long, tube-type bags made of muslin or cotton sheeting with a drawstring closure at one end.

In consistently hot states such as Texas, hunters often build in advance of the season small buildings in which they hang their deer. These resemble outhouses in size but are made of lightweight wooden frames with all walls entirely screened, which not only keep insects at bay but facilitate the circulation of breezes around the deer carcass.

In other cases it may be advisable to remove the hide (I'll discuss this in detail in the next chapter). The importance of taking off the hide in hot weather cannot be overemphasized due to the insulating qualities of the hollow hair. This is why nature has given a deer his heavy coat — to keep him warm even in bitter cold weather — and so if rapid cooling of the meat is to be achieved, off it must come. When the carcass is free of its hide and exposed to the air it will "case" or

If flies or other insects are a problem, wrap your deer with cheesecloth or sprinkle the glazed carcass with pepper.

If the weather is warm, the hide should immediately come off in camp to speed cooling of the carcass. In about eight hours, it should "case" or "glaze," forming a thin protective skin. Mike Wolter inspects his mule deer, debating whether he should slice off a tenderloin for dinner.

Using large muslin game bags for legs, quarters and other chunks of game meat is the best method when hanging elk-size animals. The porous cloth allows the circulation of air, yet keeps birds and insects off the meat. Hanging the meat bags from an overhead pole further discourages various critters from sampling your rewards. *Photo courtesy of the Browning Company*

"glaze," which is the formation of a thin, protective skinlike crust that occurs usually within about eight hours. When the casing effect is completed, the carcass should be wrapped with cheesecloth to prevent further drying of the meat and also to help keep insects from directly contacting the meat.

In the cases of larger game animals such as elk, moose, bear or others that arrive in camp not in whole form but in pieces, basically the same procedures are undertaken.

With whole legs, spend some time with your knife carefully trimming fat or tallow layers, damaged skin or bloodshot areas. However, do not use water to wash the meat. Use a dry rag to clean away any leaves, dirt smudges or other debris. If the meat has not already glazed, allow it to do so, then wrap in cheesecloth.

Other bare pieces of meat such as tenderloins, neck and brisket pieces that were transported from the field in muslin game bags should now be removed and trimmed as well. These can immediately be cut into serving-size portions and duly wrapped in plastic-coated freezer wrapping paper if you so desire. Or, if you'd prefer to wait until you are home, they can go right back into their muslin game bags and hang in a cool, shaded area.

Again, insects such as blowflies may become a problem: if given ample opportunity to contact the meat, they will lay eggs and of course ruin the meat (hunters often do not discover the damage until they arrive home when it is too late). Liberally sprinkling pepper on the meat is a good deterrent. Don't worry about it affecting the flavor of the meat because during later butchering operations it will be removed when the casing crust is trimmed away.

Meat Care on the Road

When it's time to hit the road for home, whether immediately after the kill or after several more days in camp, remember that continual cooling of your deer carcass is critical. So don't tie the deer carcass on the front hood of your automobile, where it is not only fully exposed to road grime but also subjected to engine heat.

If the only alternative is to place the deer in your trunk, absolutely do not close the lid and lock it. Make sure that the sticks keeping the body walls of the carcass spread remain in place and leave the trunk lid ajar at least 12 inches so breezes can pass through to carry out any warm air that may accumulate.

An even better idea, with conventional automobiles, is to lay the carcass on top of the trunk deck near the rear window and lash it down on both sides (pass the rope under the hinges that hold the trunk lid, or through the back windows on each side of the car). Or lay the whole deer carcass on some type of roof rack on the top of your station wagon, truck or camper. This is preferred over laying the deer directly on the roof, which prevents the circulation of air beneath the animal. Again, be sure to keep the body cavity open.

Several years ago I collected a nice buck in Colorado and due to unseasonable temperatures was faced with a three-day drive home in 80-degree heat. To ensure that my precious cargo did not spoil, I simply stopped at a gas station and purchased several bags of ice. One was pushed far up inside the chest cavity, another laid in the abdominal region, and another laid between the two hind legs in the pelvic region. I had to replace those bags of ice each time I stopped for gas, but the meat remained well chilled for the duration of the trip.

Another time I took a nice buck in South Carolina during a scorching heat spell that saw daytime temperatures near 100 degrees. The old ice bag trick again came into play, but to achieve additional cooling I did something else. On the trunk lid behind the rear window, where I would transport the deer, I placed a canvas tarp. After the deer's body cavity was filled with ice bags, I folded over the top of the tarp, tied it down and thoroughly sloshed down the canvas with cold water so that as I was driving the wind would cause the water to evaporate and render a natural cooling effect. The tarp had to be soaked each time I stopped at a gas station for more ice, and it was an inconvenience to have to untie various lashing ropes holding the tarp in place. But when I arrived home the meat actually was cold to the touch and so the effort was well worth the trouble.

If you're transporting a whole deer carcass that has had the hide removed so the meat would glaze, place the carcass in a muslin game bag to keep it clean from road grime. However, do not use the wet tarp method (still use ice bags, if necessary, inside the body cavity).

In other cases in which you have a whole deer carcass with the hide removed, it may be wise to rough-quarter the carcass in camp before undertaking a long drive home. Simply cut off the rear and front legs, neck and so on in the same manner as if you were cutting up an elk in the backcountry. Then the various cuts can be placed in plastic-coated, double-walled cardboard boxes (you can get them for free at any poultry dealer and from those fast-food restaurants that specialize in take-out chicken dinners). This is assuming the weather is cold and nature is providing the necessary refrigeration. If it's warm, use the same cardboard boxes or even camping coolers filled with ice. It is imperative, in taking this approach, that the ice be in sturdy no-leak plastic bags (double-bagging is a good idea) so that the meat will have no chance of coming in direct contact with melt water. The techniques just described are also the most desirable ways for transporting legs, quarters and other meat sections from larger game animals such as elk and moose.

When you're big-game hunting in the western states and hiring an outfitter or working out of some ranch or another, it's likely that butchering facilities will be available to hunters at the ranch head-quarters. This allows still another option for transporting meat home. Instead of doing all your meat cutting later at home, spend an extra day at the ranch doing the work, perhaps while waiting for your part-ners to fill their tags. Butcher the meat by one of the methods described in the next chapter, wrap the cuts for the freezer in portions suited to your family's needs, then pack the meat in camping coolers, styrofoam coolers, wooden crates or double-walled cardboard boxes. When you hit the road, stop in the first major city you come to and purchase dry

In extremely hot weather, precautions must be taken. When leaving Minnesota with his buck recently, the author heard a radio report of scorching-hot weather in Iowa. Before reaching it, on his way home to Ohio, he bought numerous ice bags to chill the carcass. With a water-soaked tarp placed on top, the deer remained cool.

ice to quick-freeze the meat in exactly the same way as I described for fish storage in Chapter 1.

Many other hunters, particularly those who pursue deer, antelope, elk and moose in various western states, head straight for a game-processing plant and turn their animals over to professional meat cutters. These storage lockers and meat-processing plants do the entire job of butchering game animals, wrapping the various cuts of meat, even grinding burger and sausage from the trimmings, quick-freezing the meat, boxing it up and shipping it to the hunter's home. The costs of such services vary widely between processing plants and also, of course, depend upon the size of the animal in question. A mule deer may cost $75 while an elk may cost $150. Transportation costs must be added (airfreight charges run in the neighborhood of $25 per 100 pounds). To some, this may seem like a good deal, especially if they are not so dedicated to hunting as to insist upon doing their own butchering, or if money is no object. But several other factors may enter the picture.

First, it is becoming increasingly common for big-game hunters to farm out such work, only to discover when the box of meat packages is later sent to them that they are, curiously, a little short in many of the prime roasts and tenderloins. A beginning hunter who has just killed his first deer or elk may not notice the shortage because he doesn't really know what or how much to expect. But the veteran hunter will know! This isn't by any means an indictment of all game-processing plants because not all engage in such unscrupulous activities. But enough are dishonest that a high black market demand for game meat makes such "rustling" activities a growing problem.

Another reason I personally do not have a commercial plant butcher my big-game animals is because over the years I have developed certain preferences as to exactly how I want my steaks and roasts cut, and what I want done with the rest of the meat, and therefore am seldom satisfied unless I do the work myself. But "work" may be a poor term to use because I and many others look upon the effort as an enjoyable part of the total hunting experience.

6

Doing Your Own Butchering

Few thrills equal the excitement and satisfaction of bringing home a nice buck deer, and it is a special occasion indeed when the hunter claims an elk, moose or one of the other larger game animals. The hunter has every right to feel proud because outwitting big-game animals requires savvy and plenty of hard work before and during the season.

There is also a good deal of satisfaction the hunter and his family derive during the next 12 months, every time they sit down to a meal consisting of expertly cared for and prepared cuts of meat.

However, while it is common for sportsmen to eagerly tackle the business of filleting a fish or plucking a pheasant, it is just as common for them to feel absolutely overwhelmed by a deer carcass. It is the enormous size of some big-game animals that instills this uncertainty and trepidation, but this need not happen. Butchering big-game animals, while admittedly more complicated than cleaning a catch of bluegills, merely involves a number of manual, step-by-step procedures that anyone can quickly learn.

I don't mean to belittle the matter but it's worth mentioning that even a hunter's children can easily handle many of the meat-cutting operations once they've been shown how a time or two. In fact, it's a good experience for them. With all the garbage that kids are being taught in the schools these days, and the anti-hunting propaganda seen on television, watching an animal butchered, and even helping, gives them a realistic perspective as to where their food comes from. This is a valuable and meaningful education that kids from non-hunting or non-farming families are not likely ever to acquire; unfortunately, these very children are the ones most likely to grow up professing anti-hunting values. So if your kids ever want to watch you butcher a deer, by all means let them. And if they ask to help, gladly give them the opportunity and in years to come you may have hunting partners for life.

As to a hunter's own doubts regarding the successful butchering of his first big-game animal, here's a worthwhile suggestion. Instead of looking at that huge carcass hanging from the garage rafters, and not knowing exactly where to begin, try tackling the job piecemeal. That is, remove one piece of meat that is relatively easy to handle, such as a front leg, take it into the house and thoroughly reduce it to wrapped cuts of meat for the freezer. Then go back to the garage and get another front leg and handle that, momentarily forgetting about all the rest. Since you've already just finished a front leg, and learned a little something, this second one should be a snap. Then do a rear leg, and soon the carcass won't seem so large and forbidding.

As in the case of field-dressing a deer or other big-game animal, advance planning will save time and make everything go smoothly. So, before allowing your knife blade to touch the carcass for the first time, prepare your work site and assemble the various supply items and equipment you'll need.

You'll need two knives and either a whetstone or some type of sharpening steel. One of the knives can be the same hunting model you used to field-dress your deer; the other should be a "boning" knife. I use a common fish fillet knife because its thin, flexible blade easily bends to follow the contours of bones.

You may or may not need a saw to cut bones, depending upon the butchering method you decide upon (as described later). I personally don't like the use of saws, except for such chores as removing the lower legs or cutting through the neck bone. But should you prefer to use a saw, try to borrow a professional meat saw from a friend (they are far too expensive to buy). If this isn't possible, use a conventional hacksaw with a new blade.

Buy or borrow some type of meat grinder. A simple cast-iron, hand-crank model with an assortment of cutting blades can be purchased in most housewares stores for less than $15 and with a modicum of care it should last a lifetime. These models attach to the edge of something, like a picnic table or kitchen counter, by a thumb screw which is turned until the device is securely mounted on the working surface.

Since using a hand-crank meat grinder can require a lot of effort (involving, again, the venerable Armstrong method), hunters who take their deer every year, and occasionally some other big-game animal, eventually invest in an electric grinder. These models generally cost $75 to $100 but they are wise investments. From my experience, they won't necessarily do the job any better than a hand-crank model, but they will do it in only a fraction of the time. With an electric model you'll also receive various cutting attachments, plus a casing stuffer for making link sausage.

You'll need approximately two rolls of aluminum foil, two rolls of plastic-coated freezer wrapping paper, a small roll of masking tape, a small roll of cotton string and a felt-tipped marking pen. This will suffice for an average-size whitetail, mule deer, blacktail or antelope. If the animal to be butchered is an elk or moose, obtain six rolls of foil and wrapping paper.

Another item of advance planning is reserving an order of beef suet. Fat or tallow is required in the grinding of burger and sausage, yet that from deer and other big-game animals is not at all tasteful and is trimmed away and discarded. So a quantity of beef suet (for a deer, 10 pounds is sufficient; obtain 25 pounds if you have an elk or moose) is substituted. Beef suet is very inexpensive – the going price in most supermarkets is about 25 cents per pound; if you do your shopping in a small, family-owned store you may be able to get the suet for free. In any event, it's necessary to put in your order for suet early, because about midway through the deer season there will suddenly be a drain on the amount of suet available, due to other hunters wanting tallow to do their meat grinding as well. So reserve in advance the quantity of suet you think you'll need. If you don't collect your deer and have to cancel your suet order, the butcher will easily be able to sell it to someone else.

Lastly, in getting ready to do your butchering, you'll need a wide counter space to work on for about eight hours (for an average-size deer) and some type of cutting board also is very helpful. If there is no such space available in your kitchen, a picnic table carried into your garage is fine. Or you can lay a sheet of plywood on top of sawhorses in your basement. For cleanliness, cover the top of the working surface with a long sheet or two of freezer paper, taped down around the edges.

Aging Big-Game Meat

You've arrived home with a splendid deer and are thinking about getting the butchering operation under way. But wait! Back up just a bit and consider whether you should allow the venison to age. Aging is nothing more than allowing the meat to hang for a prescribed length

Before butchering your big game, you may want to age the meat. Although aging imparts tenderness and additional flavor, it is not necessary if your game has already hung in camp several days before heading home. The author took this fine buck in southern Ohio's Wayne National Forest.

of time while being subjected to cold (not freezing!) air temperatures. When this is undertaken, desirable bacterial organisms work to break down the meat fibers and tissues, which makes the meat far more tender and flavorful.

Ideally, big-game animals should age at a temperature of 38 to 40 degrees for a period of four to six days. If the temperature is a bit colder than this in the morning and slightly warmer in the afternoon, that is okay. Just ensure that the meat is not allowed to freeze or hang in midday temperatures exceeding 48 to 50 degrees.

Keep in mind that home aging of big-game meat is recommended only if you live in a western state where you hunt mule deer or elk relatively close to home, or if you hunt whitetails somewhere in the East or Midwest and are returning home shortly after the kill. If your deer or other big-game animal has already undergone two or three days aging as it hung in camp, then another two or three days while you were on the road traveling home, additional home aging is neither necessary nor recommended.

The perfect location for hanging venison to age involves several requisites. The place should be shady for the greater part of the day, a bit breezy if possible, and protected so that the neighbor's dog isn't able to invite himself to dinner. A garage or shed possessing a door you can close is ideal, but even an open-air carport may work if your neighbors don't have pets.

If the venison you plan to age is from a large-game animal such as a moose, and the meat was brought home in cloth bags, remove the legs and hang them separately (they should already have a casing glaze to protect them). Then remove smaller meat chunks such as neck meat, backstraps and so on from the cloth bags, wrap in cheesecloth, then return them to the game bags for hanging. If flies become a problem, sprinkle pepper on the outsides of the bags.

If the deer you brought home has already had the hide removed, simply hang the glazed carcass as-is to age, unless insects become bothersome and then you'll want to slip a game bag over the carcass.

If the deer you brought home still has the hide intact, you'll have to determine whether to remove the hide immediately or leave it on during the aging period. Weather is the deciding factor here. If it's quite cold the hide can be left on, but if it's warm it should come off as soon as possible.

However, even when it's cold there is a lot to be said in favor of removing the animal's hide the very minute it is practical to do so, provided the hide is not required to protect the meat during the course of transportation activities. If nothing else, the hide peels away very easily when it is still fresh and "green." After it has remained on the animal for several days, and begun to dry and harden, the job of removing the hide requires considerably more effort.

In very warm climates, such as the desert Southwest or the tropical regions of the deep South, it may be impossible to naturally age venison outdoors. In this situation, I like to remove the animal's hide and attend to all butchering chores as quickly as possible. However, after the cuts of meat are wrapped and labeled, I don't immediately transfer them to the freezer. Instead, I stack them on the lower shelves in my refrigerator, where they sit and age for about four days in 38-degree temperatures. Then they go into the deep freezer.

Removing the Hide

Several times I've mentioned removing the hide from a deer or other big-game animal. Whether the operation is accomplished in camp, at home prior to aging, or at home after aging, you should now probably take a closer look at the best way to accomplish the task.

First, if at all possible, the animal should be hanging. In this manner, as the hide is removed, it falls down and away from the carcass so that hair, dust and other debris are not allowed to contact the meat. I personally like to hang the animal by the hind legs.

Begin by making a shallow cut entirely around the neck, just below the ears and chin. Next, extend the abdominal cut you made when field dressing by going right down the centerline of the chest to the cut made around the neck (there's no need to cut ribs; simply guide the blade up and over the sternum or breast bone, cutting only hide). From the centerline cut, make perpendicular cuts that go down the inside of each front leg to the knee, then make circular cuts that go all around the knees. Finally, make additional perpendicular cuts from

In removing the hide, most expert hunters use their knives minimally. Instead, they roll the hide into a cylinder as they push down with their knuckles and separate it from the carcass.

the pelvic region down the insides of each hind leg, and again circular cuts around each knee.

In making all of these cuts, use just the tip of your knife with the blade edge facing up, so the meat directly underneath the hide is not damaged.

It's now an easy task to begin freeing the hide from the carcass, with a minimum of additional cutting. In fact, you may only have to use a knife at first, around the tail region to create a flap of skin, in

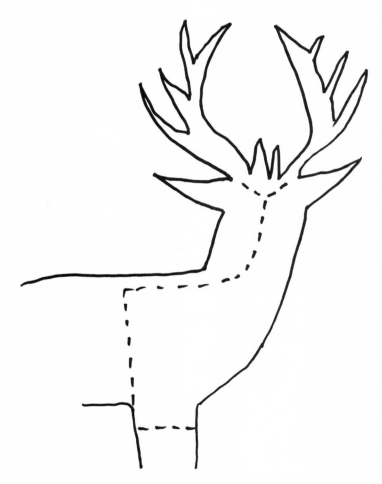

If you desire to have a head mount, above all do not cut the neck or throat skin. Leave a wide cape for the taxidermist to work with, making your knife cuts as shown here.

certain places around the legs and brisket, or anywhere that the skin has become hardened. The remainder of the hide removal is done with the hands, almost like peeling a tough banana. Grab the flap of hide you've cut away in the vicinity of the tail, roll it just a bit if necessary for a good grip, then with the weight of your body begin pushing downward with your knuckles. As part of the hide begins to separate from the carcass, it can be rolled even more for a firmer grasp and therefore additional leverage. This technique helps prevent accidental slices into the meat that even an expert skinner might incur if he used a knife continually.

Another method of hide removal is rapidly gaining in popularity with many hunters, particularly those who are members of hunting clubs that stage drives and often account for several big-game animals all at once. I first learned of this method when hunting with the Fort Mott Deer Hunting Club near Summerton, South Carolina. There, steeped in rich Southern tradition, hunt clubs use redbone and bluetick hounds to drive deer through jungle-like swamps to hunters waiting on stand. It's about the only way to successfully move the deer out of the thick tropical habitat where, if their numbers are not regularly thinned, the whitetails quickly over-populate their range and in huge herds begin devastating nearby farmers' croplands. To accomplish the beneficial herd reduction, South Carolina allows a six-month deer season and hunters are permitted, in many regions, to take one buck per day!

Anyway, when I was recently invited as a guest to hunt with the Fort Mott Club, we accounted for eight whitetails the first day. That is a lot of deer to skin, even when there are numerous volunteers to help with the work. But the Fort Mott Club members have devised a unique method of stripping hides from big-game animals using nothing more than a chain and a pickup truck. And attesting to the efficiency of the method, it's worth noting that those eight whitetails were all skinned perfectly in a total time span of less than 30 minutes!

A deer is hung in the usual manner, and the initial cuts made through the hide as I described before; that is, the neck cut is made, then the abdominal cut extended to the neck, perpendicular cuts made down the insides of the legs, then cuts made around each of the knees.

Next, the animal is lowered to the ground and laid upon a sheet of cardboard or plywood that has a clean surface. A chain is then used to hold the animal firmly by the head to some immovable object. We

If you want to have the hide tanned, lay it out flat and trim away all tissue remnants, as well as every bit of fat. Then rub the hide thoroughly with salt, roll it into a cylinder, tie with string, and store in a cool, dry location until you can deliver it to a taxidermist.

wrapped the chain around the head of the deer and then around the base of a telephone pole.

Next, with your knife, cut back about six or eight inches of hide at the back of the neck to create a large flap. Underneath this flap place a golf ball (or stone of similar size). Then with a hank of stout rope make a small noose, slip it over the lump of neck hide with the golf ball underneath, snug the noose up tightly, then tie the opposite end of the rope to the rear bumper of a nearby vehicle.

The driver then begins pulling away, and as he drives off (slow and easy!) the hide quickly strips from the animal. It is absolutely amazing. The hide isn't damaged one bit, and there are no accidental knife slashes anywhere on the carcass. It is as clean as a whistle.

I've since used this technique several times when hunting back home and always marvel at its efficiency. The method will work with any big-game animal. Some Pennsylvania friends tell me they even use the method when skinning their black bears to avoid handling the greasy beasts too much.

After the hide is removed, I recommend hoisting the animal into the air by the hind legs if it is not already so positioned. Then, use your hacksaw to remove all four lower legs just below the knees (be extremely careful you don't cut either of the Achilles tendons of the rear legs, or the carcass will fall to the ground). Remove the head by cutting down through the neck meat just behind the ears until you reach the neck bone, then either cut through the neck bone with your saw or twist the head free.

Easy Meat-Cutting Methods

I've mentioned several times that I dislike using a saw for butchering, except for cutting off the lower legs or cutting through the neck bone. Instead, I bone out all of the various cuts of meat, and with good reason. First, boneless meat doesn't require nearly as much freezer space. Also, sawing the bones of big-game animals produces countless little specks of marrow "dust" and chips that find themselves liberally sprinkled throughout the meat near where the cuts were made. And unlike the marrow in the bones of beef steers or hogs, that contained in wild-game bones imparts a flavor many do not like. Other hunters strongly disagree and, as in the case of beef and pork, like bones as part of their steaks, chops and other cuts. For this reason I'll describe two different butchering methods to accommodate the preferences of both camps. I suggest you try both ways, half the deer done by one method, the other half the other way. Accurately label your wrapped packages so you know which is which, and as you eat your venison decide upon which method you prefer.

Hunters who have a liking for steaks or chops instead of boneless tenderloin steaks will want to use this first method, which requires a bit of bone cutting.

First, cut off the entire neck meat by making your knife cut from the base of the throat to the beginning of the brisket, then lifting, cutting and separating the meat from the bone. When laid out flat on your cutting table, this should give you a large rectangular piece of meat. Since this meat is not so tender and is laced with sinew, I like to cut the meat from the back of the neck into one-inch cubes to use in soups and stews. The lower neck meat goes for sausage and burger (which I'll describe how to make later).

Second, saw right down the middle of the backbone from the front shoulder to the tail and the carcass will fall away into right and left sides.

Third, with a "side" lying on your flat work surface, make a vertical cut from just behind the front leg to the area of the back where the tenderloin begins (just behind the front shoulder). With your boning knife, carefully separate the shoulder roast from the bone until you have a wide slab of meat. This can be rolled up into a cylinder, tied securely in about six places with cotton string, then sliced in half to provide two rolled shoulder roasts. The lower portion around the brisket, and also the foreleg, go for stew meat and either sausage or burger.

Fourth, using your saw again, make an angular cut that goes from the middle of the rib cage to a point just about where the tail was previously located. (As you traverse the hind leg at this point, use your knife to first cut down into the meat, then the saw to cut the part of the pelvic girdle located beneath.) The upper, lengthy section of meat this provides can then be laid flat on your work surface, and with vertical saw cuts the various steaks or chops are produced. Some hunters prefer a wide front portion to serve as a standing rib roast, followed by five or six inch-thick chops; others prefer the entire back region to

Cutting off the lower legs is easy with a hacksaw. This is the only bone cutting the author recommends, because sawing lets distasteful marrow dust contact the meat.

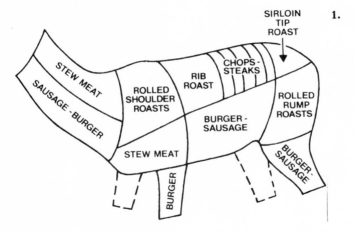

1.

1. There are two ways to butcher a big-game animal. The first method, shown here, produces steaks and roasts but requires bone cutting down the middle of the back.

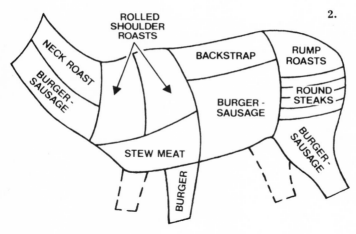

2.

2. With the second method, hunters obtain roasts and tenderloins. Why not try both methods, plainly label your meat packages, then later decide which procedure you like best?

go into eight or nine steaks. The pyramid-shaped piece of meat remaining at the tail is the sirloin tip roast.

Fifth, the lower section of meat, beneath the steaks, contains the remainder of the short ribs which can be carefully trimmed for sausage or burger.

Sixth, this leaves the rest of the hind leg. As with the front legs, the lower back legs contain much sinew and ligaments and are best reserved for grinding into burger or sausage.

Seventh, the rump, as with the front shoulder, can be carefully separated from the bone to leave a thick, wide piece of meat that can be rolled, tied with string and sliced into roasts of the size your family requires.

The second method requires no bone cutting with a saw.

First, the neck is removed the same as before and it can go for stew meat and either sausage or burger. However, I often like to remove the upper portion back of the neck, roll it and tie it into neck roasts.

Second, the front shoulder, brisket and lower leg, as before, go into rolled shoulder roasts, stew meat and burger, respectively.

A backstrap has just been removed. These are the tenderest parts of any big-game animal. They can be broiled whole, but the author favors butterflying them into thick, sumptuous filet mignons.

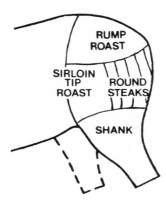

There is a difference of opinion regarding the locations of and methods of cutting sirloin tip roasts and round steaks. Some hunters contend the sirloin tip is at the very end of the rump, high along the back. Others refer to the large, oval muscle toward the front of each rear leg as the sirloin tip roast. Also, as shown here, round steaks may be sliced either vertically or horizontally. Choose the particular method you like best.

Third, instead of sawing down the middle of the backbone, then making vertical cuts to produce chops and steaks with bones, I like to remove the entire backstrap in one long piece. It lies adjacent to the backbone, running from just behind the front shoulder to where the front of the rear leg begins, and rests in a type of pocket created by the offset vertebrae where they meet the ribs. Insert your fillet knife just behind the front shoulder, so the blade lies flat against the backbone, then carefully guide it all the way along the length of the backbone to the rear leg. Now, at the shoulder, make a perpendicular cut about four inches in length. It then is an easy matter to gently cut and lift, cut and lift some more, until the backstrap is finally removed for its entire length. Many hunters like to freeze these backstraps whole, to be broiled over coals later when there are many dinner guests. I prefer to produce inch-thick filet mignon steaks by making "butterfly" cuts as follows: lay the backstrap on your working surface and, beginning one inch from either end, slice the meat vertically but not all the way through; then, on the next one-inch slice, do cut all the way through. This enables you to fold over the two side-by-side portions with the connecting hinge in the middle, to create a much larger steak than if you simply reduced the entire backstrap to inch-thick slices.

Fourth, an important thing to remember in using this particular butchering technique is that directly beneath the backstrap, located *inside* the body cavity, are two mini-tenderloins, one lying on each side of the backbone. In the previous butchering method, with vertical saw cuts to produce chops and steaks, these are included in the meat portions obtained, but not so when the backstrap is removed intact by the second method. Simply reach inside the body cavity and with your fillet knife pluck them out. Each is about 1½ inches thick by 12 inches in length. Do this work gently, because these sections of meat are so tender they almost fall apart in your hands. They should have a rather crusted glaze on them, which can be trimmed somewhat if you like, but this is entirely optional and most hunters like to broil the tenderloins as-is and trim away the crust at the table.

Fifth, directly below the backstrap, clean the meat from the ribs for burger or sausage.

Sixth, all that is left now on the side of the deer you're working on is the entire hind leg. I like to remove the upper portion from the pelvic bone, cut it into roasts and tie each with string. From the meat just below you can slice several nice round steaks. Cut the meat about one-inch thick with your knife until you reach the leg bone, which you can cut with a saw if you prefer; I like, instead, to remove this entire slab of meat intact, remove the entire bone with my fillet knife, then slice the round steaks.

Tying venison roasts is easy. If you have a relatively large slab of meat, you can roll it into a cylinder as with the front shoulder meat, tie it in numerous places, then cut roasts compatible with your fam-

Tying rolled rump roasts is easy. Cut large slabs of meat, roll them, and tie with cotton string. Or lay irregular pieces of meat side by side and tie them together. Then trim with your knife to produce professional-looking cuts.

ily's needs. You will likely have accumulated several irregularly shaped chunks of meat that can be laid side-by-side and on top of each other, then securely tied into whole roasts. Use clean cotton string and the surgeon's tie, which consists of a double-overhand knot followed by a single-overhand. The initial double-overhand grips the meat snugly and will not slip, allowing you to cinch up the knot with the final single-overhand.

Each cut of meat should first be wrapped in aluminum foil or clear plastic Saran wrap. Press the material firmly around all sides of the meat to eliminate air pockets; otherwise, freezer air will gradually seep in and dry out the meat. Follow the first wrap with a second covering of plastic-coated freezer wrapping paper for additional protection, using the popular drugstore fold. Seal all edges with masking tape. Last, use a felt-tipped marking pen to label each package as to the cut of meat inside, its approximate weight and the date it was frozen. This will eliminate a lot of guesswork many months later when you are rummaging around in your freezer with thoughts of a venison dinner in mind.

During all of these various meat-cutting activities you'll have slowly accumulated many scraps and pieces of meat that should have been saved in a large bowl or even a clean cardboard box. I even like to go back over the bony skeleton and spend as much time as is necessary to remove every speck of meat remaining. Pay particular attention to the meat lying along the backbone and in the vicinity of the pelvis as this produces the tenderest sausage and burger.

There are sure to be additional trimmings that are less desirable for human consumption, especially that meat which is found between the ribs and on the lower legs. I never discard this meat, even though I won't be eating it, because it's still valuable.

I make dog food! It's really quite a sensible idea when you consider it's almost pure protein, and if you have hunting dogs or other pets you'll save a good deal of money on their feed during the upcoming year. To make the dog food, I simply cut these less desirable scraps into one-inch pieces, then throw them all into a big five-gallon pot on the stove. Add just enough water to barely cover the meat, but nothing else. Then put on the lid and let the works slowly bubble for a few hours until the meat is thoroughly cooked. Next, let the pot cool, then begin ladling the meat and broth into plastic freezer containers (I like the kind that hold about two cups and have snap-on lids). Label these containers after they are filled, then stack them in your freezer. Generally, I don't feed this venison "stew" straight but give my Brittany one container mixed with an equal quantity of conventional dry dog food. The venison doesn't have to be heated (but make sure it's completely defrosted) before mixing it with the dry food.

All of this makes good conservation sense because you're not only putting every possible bit of the deer to good use but saving a lot of money in the process.

An important step in game-cutting operations is removing every possible bit of fat. It does not freeze well and, unlike the fat of domesticated livestock, is distasteful.

Grinding Burger and Sausage

We've already mentioned that every serious hunter should buy, borrow or beg either a hand-crank or electric meat grinder. Both types operate in basically the same way. Meat trimmings are fed into the top mouth of the grinder and then the handle turned or the electric switch turned on. The front of the grinder has a removable faceplate, underneath which are interchangeable disks with holes of various sizes. There also is a four-bladed cutting disk.

This arrangement allows a hunter to coarse-grind the meat first, then feed it through the grinder again a second or even third time, with each next smaller disk intermittently slipped into place to produce sausage or burger of various textures.

Grinding sausage and burger is enjoyable work. The amazing thing is that the finished product comes out of the grinder looking identical to that which you find neatly wrapped in plastic at the gro-

The author grinds burger with an electric grinder. Professional models cost $60 to $100 but do the work in a fraction of the time required by hand-crank grinders.

cery store. Everyone will think you had a professional butcher do your grinding for you!

From an average whitetail or mule deer you'll probably end up with approximately 25 pounds of either burger or sausage, or a combination of the two. From an elk or moose you might receive as much as 75 or 100 pounds.

There are two recipes for grinding burger that are guaranteed to please all.

Easy Burger
3 pounds venison trimmings
1 pound beef suet

For whatever quantity of burger you plan to make, use the ratio of 3 parts venison to 1 part suet. Begin by coarse-grinding the venison, then coarse-grind the beef suet. Next, on a flat work surface, thoroughly knead the two mixtures together with your hands and then coarse-grind the two together. Finally, fine-grind the mixture. We like to use this particular burger recipe just like you'd use regular hamburger when making sandwiches, spaghetti sauce, helper dinners, marzetti and so on.

Fancy Burger
3 pounds venison trimmings
1 pound beef suet
1 small onion, chopped
3 slices fresh bread, crumbled

Coarse-grind the venison trimmings, then coarse-grind the suet. Mix the two together with your hands and coarse-grind a second time. Now, knead in the onion and crumbled bread, then fine-grind the mix. This burger recipe is a bit more zesty than the previous recipe and the one we like to use when the burger is to be made into casseroles, sauces or meatloaf.

The best venison sausage recipe I've ever tasted is made as follows.

Venison Sausage
4 pounds venison trimmings
1 pound fresh, lean pork, cut into cubes
5 teaspoons salt
2½ teaspoons ground pepper
1½ teaspoons sugar
5 teaspoons sage

Coarse-grind the venison trimmings, then coarse-grind the lean pork. Thoroughly knead the two meats together until they are well mixed. Spread this coarse-ground mixture out on a flat work surface

Here is the quantity of meat packages you should expect from an average whitetail deer—a year's worth of excellent eating! Marianne Weiss prepares an inventory list before storing her bounty in the freezer.

and sprinkle the various seasonings and spices over the top. Knead again with your hands until thoroughly blended. Then run the mix through your grinder another time with the coarse disk still in place. Then grind one final time with the fine disk in place.

The above recipe results in bulk sausage, which we freeze in 1-pound packages and later make into patties for frying. We also like to crumble the sausage, fry, and use as a pizza topping or in various types of casserole dishes.

If you prefer link sausage, there is an inexpensive casing-stuffer attachment you can buy for your hand-crank grinder. (You get one of these gadgets free when you shell out the dough for a fancy electric grinder.) It is made of plastic or hard nylon and looks almost like a funnel or long spout that attaches to the front of your grinder after you've slipped in your fine-grind disk. Simply take sausage casing material, slide it over the mouth of the funnel, and as you grind, sausage fills the casing.

Sausage casings are sold on the counters of many types of grocery stores, primarily at small, independent stores who do all their own meat cutting and grinding. If the store you frequent doesn't carry casings, or have any extra to sell to you, the butcher can place an order on your behalf that you'll receive within a few days.

There are several types and sizes of sausage casings. Some consist of natural intestines from animals, others are made from edible synthetics. You can also get them in small ¾-inch diameter, all the way up to big three-inch diameters if you want to make big summer sausages or those to be hung in a smokehouse. In some cases, the casing materials have to be soaked in water first before they can be used.

When the sausage is coming from the grinder and filling the long casing tube, you'll have to twist the casing at intervals to produce the size links you desire. Sometimes I make four-inch links to use as breakfast sausages; other times I fill two- or three-foot lengths of casings to be smoked. With some types of casings you may have to tie the ends, or between the links, with cotton string to prevent the contents from spilling out until it has taken a compacted form. All of this depends upon the particular type of casings you buy. Thoroughly read any instructions that come with your casings, or follow the advice your grocer gives you. There also may be a number of sausage-stuffing tips in the instruction manual that came with your meat grinder.

7

Cooking Venison and Other Big-Game Meat

The hunter who has 75 pounds of deer meat stashed away in his freezer at the conclusion of the hunting season is very lucky indeed – even more so if it's several hundred pounds of elk, moose or other big-game meat – but not entirely because of the high cost of meat these days. On the contrary, venison is so extremely expensive that, logically, only wealthy gourmets should be able to afford it.

An explanation for this is that even the most expert deer hunter may not score every year – perhaps he'll now and then pass up smaller bucks in the hopes of something bigger coming along, and many times it never does – yet every season he nevertheless incurs many expenses. There's the general hunting license he has to buy, and in many states the special deer tag. At the outset he buys one or more firearms and frequently thereafter must stock up on ammo, targets, gun-cleaning equipment and other odds and ends. He needs hunting clothes, boots, at least one knife and mounds of accessory gear. There is the cost of food, lodging and transportation to and from the hunting site. Then there is a wealth of hidden costs, often taken for granted, like expenses for guide fees, the services of outfitters, the cost of camping equipment and much more.

Tallying up these annual expenses and then comparing them to the quantity of deer meat obtained, the insightful hunter sooner or later comes face to face with a very startling realization. Over the years, the venison he brings home probably averages out to somewhere in the neighborhood of $30 per pound!

The bottom line is that no one should ever take up deer or big-game hunting with the singular thought in mind of all that "free" meat, because there's no such thing. In the long run, it would be much cheaper to purchase 75 pounds of beef filet mignon every few months, at whatever price the butcher asks.

Aside from money matters, the hunter who regularly fills his tag is very lucky because venison is one of the most delicious and nutritious meats in the world, and also one of the most difficult to come by. Less than one percent of the world's people have the opportunity in their lifetimes to savor chops, steaks, roasts or any other cut of venison. You have 75 pounds of the stuff in your freezer every other year? You're a member of a very elite fraternity! You're royalty!

Kitchen Secrets

Big-game species are unique, because unlike many other types of meat you can't just plop a venison steak into a frypan, or slide a roast into the oven, and be guaranteed at least passable results. With venison, depending upon the chef's attitude and his culinary knowledge, the final taste test is usually either exquisite or horrid.

First, let's dispense with the gamey taste bunk commonly circulated by the ladies' magazines, those cookbook authors who live antiseptic lives in Manhattan condominiums, and other unfortunates who have failed to understand the unique qualities of venison and therefore prepared it improperly.

Venison is meat from a wild animal, usually deer, but the term also refers to meat from moose, elk and caribou. Whatever the species, it has dined upon berries, fruits, mast (nuts), agricultural crops, assorted browse (twigs, buds, leaves), vegetation (weeds, wild grasses, shrubs, moss, lichens), and numerous other foods it may randomly chance upon from time to time. Yet too many hunters and their families, not to mention many others, overlook this and make the mistake of pre-judging venison. Because it looks very much like beef, they expect it to have the flavor and texture of beef. They expect it to be very similar to fattened livestock which has been force-fed a variety of specially planted grains and grasses and then, after butchering, injected with all manner of additives, preservatives, and even artificial flavors and colors.

Further, any food product which is not commonly a regular part of any family's menu has a way of tasting different at first. The truth of the matter is that beef and other meat from domestic livestock actually is very bland. But over the years we've subconsciously accepted these characteristics. Our tastebuds have become tempered to mild eating experiences. Without really thinking about it we've come to *expect* beef, pork and even domestic fowl to be bland. If they taste otherwise upon rare occasion, our immediate suspicion is that something is wrong with the meat!

When I brought home my first deer, many years ago, the family did not think it was comparable to the quality of beef. The deer meat seemed to have too much flavor. It was too robust and rich. But those were difficult financial times for us; I was doing graduate work at Ohio University and there were two children, both still very young. So we began religiously eating the venison, like it or not. We had little choice (mainly because I had just blown about two months' worth of grocery money for deer-hunting essentials!).

Within about two weeks, however, the venison began tasting better and better. We slowly came to realize it was really very tender, juicy and flavorful. In two more weeks we had fallen head over heels in love with venison and were proclaiming to all that we liked it better than any livestock meat we had ever tasted. The meat hadn't changed at all; our tastebuds had simply become conditioned.

The following four months saw us purchase not a speck of beef, not even hamburger. Suddenly, one day I was rummaging around in the freezer looking for a roast and the last of the venison was gone! There was no alternative but to resume buying beef, and for everyone in the family, even the youngsters, those first several beef purchases were quite a disappointment. Something was lacking. The beef was tender, of course, but there was no zip to the flavor. It was the same "not right" taste sensation we had first experienced with venison. Finally, there came the inevitable conclusion: we'd have to tone down our taste preferences — not expect so much — until deer season was open once again.

Admittedly, I have tasted venison, prepared by other cooks, that was just a tad too strong even for my own likes. But this certainly is no reflection upon the quality of the meat itself. It is because the chef preparing the meal failed to trim all excess fat from the meat before cooking it. In the case of almost any game animal, it is the surface layer of fat just under the skin, and to a lesser extent the bone marrow which enters the meat when a saw is used in the butchering, that are most responsible for objectionably strong flavors. Also entering the picture, as noted earlier, are improper or delayed field-dressing procedures. Care for the meat properly in the field and when traveling home, age the meat, do minimal bone cutting or none at all, remove every speck of fat, use the right freezing techniques (which I'll discuss later), and the meat will be outstanding.

Another common error committed by sportsmen is cooking their venison too long. Grain-fed livestock is fattened considerably before being sent to market (farmers call this "finishing," and in addition to being force-fed milk and other high fat-content foods, the animals are many times physically restrained in narrow holding pens so they can't move around). These meats are consequently marbled throughout which yields an internal basting effect during the cooking process; hence, the longer (to a point) you cook beef or pork, the more tender it becomes.

Exactly the opposite is true with venison. Deer and elk do not laze around farm pastures or corrals fattening up. Their meat is extremely lean, containing very little marbling and therefore possessing minimum basting properties. As a result, the longer you cook venison (with the exceptions I'll mention shortly), the tougher it becomes.

In order to remedy the lack of internal basting, many cooks undertake special techniques. One is called "barding," and the most common example, when constructing rolled rump or shoulder roasts during the course of meat cutting, is to lay thin pieces of beef suet in the folds of the meat before completing the rolling and string-tying operations. A slightly less effective barding technique, just prior to slipping a venison roast into the oven, is draping strips of bacon over the top of the venison, the fat from which slowly melts and continually drips over the meat as it cooks.

A similar kitchen secret is called "larding," which is the injection of fats or oils into the meat. The easiest method is using an ice pick once the roast is wrapped and tied to punch holes in the meat, then cramming them with small pieces of suet which melt down and assume the tenderizing responsibilities otherwise afforded by the marbling in beef and pork roasts. More advanced cooks purchase a larding needle, available in better cookware departments. The needle looks somewhat like a huge syringe and the cylinder is filled with melted suet, lard, bacon fat or vegetable oil and then injected into the meat in many locations.

Still another ruse is using any number of moist-cooking methods

(I'll mention several later) in which the meat slowly simmers in some type of liquid or broth in a closed vessel or foil pouch, the resulting steam thereby tenderizing the meat instead of an oil or grease.

In any event, venison should practically always be cooked only to the point of what we think of in beef as medium-rare. No more! At medium-rare, it will be at its most tender, juicy and flavorful best. Forget that you may like your beefsteaks well done. *Venison is not beef*, and when cooked until well done a venison steak or roast tastes and chews like an old tractor tire.

One unique property of meat is that meat fibers and tissues have a tendency to cool very quickly. This is not such a critical concern in the case of livestock beef or pork because these meats contain so much

Since big-game meat does not possess much marbling, tenderizing techniques are recommended. "Larding," or the application of bacon or salt pork as shown here, bastes the meat externally. Another method, called "barding," is the injection of lubricants such as cooking oil or bacon fat into the meat for internal basting. Note the meat thermometer to prevent overcooking, a cardinal sin in preparing venison.

fat, which stays hot far longer than meat tissues and therefore keeps the meat warm. Yet since venison does not possess nearly the same amount of fat, even when barded or larded, it begins cooling so fast that only midway through the meal it may actually seem cold. And as venison begins cooling, it becomes tougher and tougher. Removing a venison roast from an oven, or steaks from a grill, and placing them on a cold serving platter hastens the process.

It is imperative that any cut of venison removed from the pan or oven go onto some type of pre-heated plate or warming tray. Use this simple tip and your deer meat will remain hot and juicy throughout the entire meal.

Favorite Deer Recipes

There are probably as many recipes for cooking deer meat as there are hunters who take nice bucks every year. The following recipes are

Forget that you may like your beef well done. Venison should not be cooked beyond medium-rare if it is to be tender and juicy. Always slice a roast thin, and serve on a pre-heated platter to stay warm during the meal.

the ones we rely upon most often, especially when skeptics have been invited to dinner. All are suitable for whitetails, mule deer, blacktails and related species.

Roast Venison with Bacon
1 3-pound rump roast
8 strips bacon

Use one of the tenderest rump roasts you have, taken from high on the haunch and having a minimum of connecting muscle ligaments and sinew. Place on a roasting pan and cover with bacon strips, securing them in place with toothpicks. Then insert a meat thermometer. Place the roast in an oven pre-heated to 350 degrees and cook until the thermometer needle points to "beef–rare," which should take about 1 hour. Remove to a hot serving platter and slice very thin, then slice the cooked bacon strips into little squares and sprinkle over the top. Serves four.

Venison Roast with Mushrooms
1 3-pound roast
2 cans condensed cream of mushroom soup
flour
vegetable cooking oil

For this recipe you can use a shoulder roast, neck roast, or one of your rump roasts from low on the haunch that you suspect might not be so tender if cooked by any other method. In a deep pan, heat the cooking oil until it is very hot. Dust the roast with flour, then sear it in the hot oil until it is brown on all sides (about 3 minutes). Then transfer the roast to a glass casserole baking dish. Pour over the top of the roast and around the sides the two cans of undiluted soup. Cover, place in an oven pre-heated to 400 degrees and bake 1 hour. Remove the meat to a hot serving platter and slice, then ladle the mushroom gravy over the top. Serves four.

Venison Roast with Onions
1 3-pound roast
1 envelope Lipton's dry Onion Soup Mix
¼ cup water

Pre-heat your oven to 375 degrees. Meanwhile, lay out a large square of heavy-duty aluminum foil. Place the roast in the center (a less tender cut if you prefer), then bring up the sides of the foil to form a cup. Add the water, then sprinkle the dry onion soup mix over the top of the roast. Now, bring the edges of the foil the rest of the way up and pinch them tightly together so the roast is completely enclosed in its own miniature pressure cooker. Place the foil pouch in a shallow roasting pan and bake for 1 hour. Then transfer the roast to a hot serving platter, slice thin, and pour the gravy in the bottom of the foil over the top of the meat. Serves four.

Crabapple Venison Roast
1 3-pound venison roast
½ pound salt pork
salt
ground pepper
¼ cup orange juice
2 tablespoons lemon juice
¼ teaspoon allspice

This recipe arrives courtesy of the Marlin Firearms Company and is beyond compare. Season the roast with a sprinkling of salt and pepper and cover with thin slices of the salt pork. Sear the meat in a deep, greased baking pan in an oven pre-heated to 450 degrees for 15 minutes. Reduce the heat to 350 degrees, cover the pan, and continue cooking the roast for 1 hour, basting frequently with a mixed blend of the orange juice, lemon juice and allspice. Meanwhile, prepare the glaze described below.

Crabapple Roast Glaze
2 tablespoons melted butter
2 tablespoons orange juice
½ cup crabapple jelly

Place all ingredients in a small saucepan and stir over very low heat until thoroughly blended. Thirty minutes before the roast is done, remove the salt pork. Brush the meat every 10 minutes with the glaze for the remainder of the cooking time. Transfer the meat to a hot platter and serve. Serves four.

Marinated Venison Roast

1 3-pound shoulder or neck roast
1½ cups vinegar
¾ cup vegetable oil
2 cups water
3 slices onion
1 carrot, pared and diced
2 small garlic cloves, peeled and crushed
1 teaspoon thyme
12 peppercorns
2 cloves
1 large bay leaf
1 tablespoon salt

A marinade is a liquid bath for soaking lesser cuts of meat to tenderize them and at the same time impart a subtle flavor representing the various ingredients. In a large saucepan mix all of the above ingredients (except the meat). Bring the mixture to a boil while stirring continually, then reduce the heat and simmer 15 minutes. Turn the heat off and let the marinade cool completely. Meanwhile, take your venison roast (one of the tougher cuts from the front shoulder or neck is ideal) and poke numerous holes in it with an ice pick. Place the roast in a deep glass bowl, add the marinade until the meat is entirely covered, cover the bowl, and place in your refrigerator for 24 hours. Turn the meat once every 8 hours. The following day, remove the roast, pat dry with paper toweling, dust with flour and sear on all sides in a pot containing several tablespoons of hot cooking oil. When the meat is brown, reduce the heat, add 1 cup water, cover the pot and let slow-

One exception to the rule against cooking venison beyond medium-rare is when making a pot roast that slow-simmers in a liquid for enhanced tenderness.

ly bubble for 1 hour. Slice thin and serve. Serves four. (After the roast has soaked in the marinade, it also can be prepared by any other recipe besides the one given here. Incidentally, the marinade described can be used over and over again. Simply pour it into a large glass jar with a loose-fitting lid and store in your refrigerator for up to 3 months).

Venison Pot Roast
1 3-pound roast
flour
cooking oil
4 potatoes, cut into chunks
1 onion, sliced
5 carrots, sliced thick

Flour the roast (a less tender cut if you prefer) and then sear on all sides in a pot containing several tablespoons cooking oil. Reduce the heat, add water until it comes halfway up the side of the roast, cover and let the cauldron begin bubbling slowly. After 30 minutes add the potatoes. After another 15 minutes add the carrots and onions, each time remembering to re-cover the pot. When the vegetables are tender (total cooking time will be about 1½ hours) you're ready to eat. Place the roast on a hot serving plate and slice thin. Surround the roast with the vegetables, then pour the gravy from the bottom of the pan over everything. For variety, try occasionally adding 1 can of green beans or 1 can of mushrooms to the other vegetables. These should go in at the same time you add the carrots and onions. Serves four.

Venison Stroganoff
1½ pounds venison, cubed
flour
½ cup butter or margarine
1 clove garlic, minced
1 onion, chopped
1 tablespoon salt
¼ teaspoon pepper
1½ cups water
1 cup mushrooms
1¼ cups sour cream

Flour the venison cubes (use your less tender stew meat) and brown them in a frypan in the butter along with the minced garlic. Add the onion, salt and pepper. Stir in the water and simmer slowly, covered, for 45 minutes. Now add the mushrooms and sour cream and continue to cook 15 minutes, but do not allow the mixture to come to a boil. We like to serve this over a bed of thick Pennsylvania Dutch noodles, but for variety use rice or mashed potatoes. Serves four.

West Texas Fried Venison

2 pounds venison steaks, cut 1-inch thick
¼ cup flour
1 teaspoon salt
¼ teaspoon black pepper
5 tablespoons bacon fat
1 stalk celery, cut in pieces
3 medium onions, sliced thin
2 tablespoons Worcestershire Sauce
2 cups tomatoes (from can, with packing liquid)
8 ounces wide noodles

This sumptuous recipe also comes from the kitchens of the Marlin Firearms Company and is a special treat indeed. For the venison, we use round steak cut from the hind leg, or you can slice up a rump roast. Cut the steak meat into serving-size, 8-ounce pieces. Mix the flour, salt and pepper and thoroughly dredge the meat pieces. Heat the bacon fat in a deep skillet and brown the meat on all sides. Add the celery and onions and cook until they are just slightly brown. Add the other ingredients, cover the pan, reduce the heat and cook slowly until the meat is tender (1½ hours). Serve over a bed of noodles prepared separately. Serves four.

Fried Tenderloin

4 inch-thick tenderloins, "butterflied"
cooking oil

This amazingly simple recipe is one of the best I've ever tasted. Add ⅛ inch cooking oil to a cast-iron skillet and heat until it is very hot. Add the tenderloins, sear on one side for 2 or 3 minutes, then flip them to fry the other side. Make sure they are not cooked beyond medium-rare. Serve as-is, or each with 2 tablespoons mushrooms sautéed in butter. Serves four.

Broiled Venison
venison steaks, or large backstrap strip
Worcestershire Sauce

Another incredibly easy yet tasty way to prepare the tenderest cuts of venison is by broiling over charcoal the same as you would beefsteaks. Use venison steaks cut from the backbone, or broil large sections of backstrap. Cook only until medium-rare, sprinkling occasionally with the Worcestershire Sauce. Count on an inch-thick steak for each person, or 8 ounces of backstrap meat sliced very thin.

Joe Brunneti's Liver and Heart
  1 pound deer liver
  1 pound deer heart
  2 eggs, beaten
  1 cup flour
  1 tablespoon garlic powder
  ½ teaspoon sweet basil
  ½ teaspoon sage

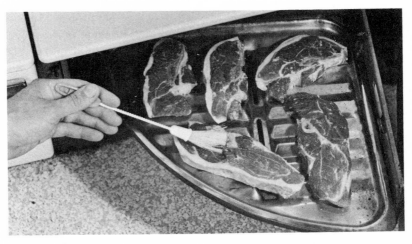

Broiling is an excellent method of preparing steaks from all big-game animals. Be sure not to overcook, and frequently baste with drippings or bacon fat.

Soak the liver and heart in salted water for 24 hours, then remove and pat dry with paper toweling. Slice the liver and heart into ⅜-inch thick strips. In a bowl, beat the eggs. Mix the flour, garlic powder and sweet basil, on a plate, until they are thoroughly blended. Dip the strips of meat in the beaten egg, dredge with the seasoning mix, then place in a cast-iron skillet containing several tablespoons of hot cooking oil. Fry on medium-high heat until the liver and heart are just barely pink inside (no longer!). During the final few minutes of cooking, lightly sprinkle the meat with the sage. Serves four.

Deer Hunter's Stew

3 pounds venison, cut into cubes
1 teaspoon salt
½ teaspoon pepper
cooking oil
water
3 potatoes, cut into chunks
2 onions, sliced
6 carrots, sliced thick
1 can green beans

Flour the venison cubes (or stew-meat pieces) and then brown them in a skillet containing several tablespoons of cooking oil. Transfer the meat to a deep pot and add all the remaining ingredients. Add water until the contents of the pot are just barely covered. Simmer slowly on low heat for 3 hours. If you like, stir in a few pinches of flour 5 minutes before serving to thicken the gravy. Serves four.

Venison Meatloaf

2 pounds deerburger
2 eggs
3 slices fresh bread, crumbled
¾ cup milk
1¼ tablespoons prepared mustard
5 tablespoons ketchup
1 tablespoon mixed Italian herbs
1 medium onion, chopped
1 medium green pepper, chopped
1 tablespoon salt

In a large bowl, beat the eggs and stir in the milk. Add the remaining ingredients and thoroughly knead with your hands. Form into a bread-loaf shape and place in an ungreased loaf pan. Place this pan in a shallow, flat-cake pan holding about an inch of boiling water and bake in a pre-heated 375 degree oven for 2 hours. Serves four.

Chesterhill Farm Chili

2 pounds deerburger
1 green pepper, chopped
2 16-ounce cans red kidney beans with liquid
2 12-ounce cans tomato sauce
1 tablespoon red cayenne pepper
2 tablespoons garlic powder
1 teaspoon cumin seed
4 tablespoons chili powder
2 bay leaves, broken
cooking oil

We've tried dozens of chili recipes but the one that remains our favorite was invented on our combination farm and game preserve in southern Ohio, where we frequently see as many as 12 whitetails at one time on our south meadow. Brown the deerburger in a skillet containing several tablespoons of cooking oil. When the meat is cooked, spoon off the fat drippings, then transfer the meat to a deep pot. Add the remaining ingredients, cover, and simmer on low heat for 2 hours. This chili (we often make several gallons at a time) is especially good when reheated the next day or after being in the freezer several months. Let each person salt to his own taste.

Deer MacPepper

1½ quarts Chesterhill Farm Chili
1 7-ounce package macaroni
8 green peppers, sliced lengthwise into halves
1 cup grated cheddar cheese
½ teaspoon salt
⅛ teaspoon black pepper
½ teaspoon oregano
½ cup Parmesan cheese

Around our place, this delicious recipe is popular when we have leftover chili. Cook the macaroni according to the package instructions, then drain. Remove stem and core-seeds from peppers and slice lengthwise into halves. Add the peppers to a large pot of boiling salted water for 2 minutes, then quickly remove and drain. Meanwhile, heat the chili, then stir in the cooked macaroni, half the cheddar cheese and the seasonings. Stuff the pepper halves with the chili-macaroni mix. Sprinkle on top the remaining cheddar cheese, then sprinkle on the Parmesan cheese. Next, arrange the stuffed peppers on a large cookie sheet, then slip under your oven's broiler for 3 minutes. Serves eight.

Elk, Moose, Antelope and Bear Recipes

As with fish, many big-game recipes are interchangeable, so feel free to use any of the previous deer recipes when preparing steaks, roasts and burger from elk, moose, caribou and antelope. Bear meat tastes very similar to beef, but like pork requires longer cooking times to be completely safe from the remote possibility of trichinosis, so use appropriate slow-cooking methods for the bruins.

The following are recipes intended specifically for the largest big-game species.

Moose Casserole
2 pounds moose meat, cubed
1 can condensed cream of mushroom soup
1 cup canned tomatoes, with packing liquid
1 envelope Lipton's dry Onion Soup Mix

Arrange the meat cubes in the bottom of a large glass casserole dish. Pour the mushroom soup (undiluted) over the top. Sprinkle on the dry onion soup mix, then pour the tomatoes over the top. Cover the dish and bake slowly at 325 degrees for 2 hours. Serves four.

Bagged Elk or Moose Roast
1 3-pound elk or moose roast
1 medium onion, quartered
2 bay leaves, crumbled
1 teaspoon salt
½ teaspoon black pepper
½ cup dry red wine
1 large Brown-in-Bag

Buy a 10"×16" plastic Brown-in-Bag made for oven roasting at your grocery store. Shake 1 tablespoon of flour inside the bag and then place in a deep roasting pan. Pour the wine into the bag and stir with the flour until well mixed. Rub the meat with the salt and pepper and then set inside the bag. Arrange the onion pieces and bay leaves around the roast, then close the bag with a wire twist-tie. Make several half-inch slits in the top of the bag, then bake 2½ hours in an oven pre-heated to 325 degrees. Slice thin and serve on a hot plate. Serves four.

This is Stuffed Holiday Moose, made from a round steak rolled into a cylinder with stuffing inside. Superb!

Stuffed Holiday Moose

1 large, wide, ¾-inch thick moose round steak
3 cups breadcrumbs
¼ cup flour
1 medium onion, chopped
1 stalk celery, chopped
½ cup butter
1 green pepper, chopped
½ teaspoon paprika
½ teaspoon salt
¼ teaspoon black pepper
bacon strips

Mix the salt, pepper and flour. Trim the steak until it is square and then thoroughly pound in the flour mixture with a wooden meat mallet. Mix all the remaining ingredients except the bacon strips to create a stuffing, sprinkling in a bit of water as necessary so it is not too dry. Lay this stuffing on top of the round steak, then roll the steak into a type of cylinder and tie with cotton string. Set the rolled, stuffed steak in a shallow roasting pan and completely cover with bacon strips. Bake for 1 hour in an oven pre-heated to 325 degrees or until the meat is tender. Serves four.

Moose Swiss Steak

1 moose (or elk) round steak, about 2½ pounds
flour
cooking oil
1 can condensed tomato soup
3 cups water
2 teaspoons salt
1 teaspoon black pepper
3 stalks celery, cut into thick pieces
1 medium onion, chopped
1 large green pepper, chopped
¼ teaspoon sweet basil
2 tablespoons Worcestershire Sauce

Lay the round steak out flat, then prick thoroughly with a fork. Cut the steak into 8-ounce serving-size pieces and dredge them thoroughly with flour. Brown the pieces in a skillet containing hot cooking oil. Arrange the pieces of meat in a large glass casserole or baking dish and add 2 cups of the water and the salt and pepper. Cover the dish and bake 2 hours in an oven pre-heated to 325 degrees. Mix the tomato soup (undiluted) with the remaining cup of water and pour over the meat. Add the remaining ingredients, cover again, and continue baking 1 hour longer until the meat is tender. Remove the meat to a hot plate. Sprinkle a bit of flour or cornstarch into the liquid in the bottom of the baking dish and stir continuously to thicken the gravy, which can then be ladled over the meat. Serves four.

Antelope Surprise
1 2-pound antelope roast
½ cup flour
¼ cup honey
4 tablespoons butter or margarine
3 cups sour cream
½ teaspoon salt
¼ teaspoon black pepper

Slice the antelope roast in half to create two equal, thick slabs. Flour these slabs well, then brown in a skillet containing the melted butter, to which has been added 2 tablespoons cooking oil to prevent the butter from clarifying. Add 1½ cups of the sour cream to the bottom of a large glass baking dish, then arrange the two slabs of antelope on top of the sour cream and sprinkle on the salt and pepper. Pour the honey over the top of the meat, cover the casserole dish and bake for 1 hour in an oven pre-heated to 300 degrees. Remove the lid and add the remaining sour cream, then cover and continue baking 30 minutes longer or until the meat is tender. Serves four.

Tomatoed Bear Steak
1 2-pound bear steak
3 tablespoons tomato sauce
1½ cups canned beef broth
1 cup red wine
1 large onion, diced
⅛ teaspoon thyme
½ cup flour
4 tablespoons bacon fat

Use a thick round steak cut from the rear leg of a black bear, or a boneless shoulder or rump roast no more than 2 inches thick. With a wooden mallet, pound the flour into the steak. Sauté the onions in the bacon fat until they are clear, then brown the meat on both sides in the same fat. Add half the wine and half the beef broth and bring to a boil, then reduce the heat slightly and continue to cook 5 minutes. Turn the steak, reduce the heat to a simmer and continue cooking, covered, for 1½ hours. When the steak is tender, remove it to a warm platter. Add the tomato sauce and the remaining wine and broth to

Bear is one big-game meat that should always be well cooked. As with pork, there is the remote chance that trichinosis could be a problem with rare meat. This bear roast with tomato sauce simmers in a cast-iron Dutch oven.

the juices remaining in the pan and stir to create a smooth sauce. Ladle the sauce over the bear steak and serve. Serves four.

Appled Bear with Kraut
2 pounds bear meat, sliced ½-inch thick
1 pound sauerkraut
1 large apple, diced finely
½ cup sour cream
½ cup dry white wine
1 medium onion, finely diced
1 teaspoon salt
¼ teaspoon black pepper
½ teaspoon paprika
bacon fat

Use round steak from the hind leg. Brown the sliced strips of meat on all sides in a skillet containing several tablespoons of bacon fat. Remove the meat temporarily and add the onions and cook until they are clear. Add the salt, pepper and paprika, stirring well. Then add the meat again to the pan, pour the wine over the top, cover the pan and simmer slowly until the liquid has almost entirely evaporated, which will take about 45 minutes, or until the meat is tender. Heat the sauerkraut in a saucepan, then drain off the liquid and stir in the diced apple. Stir this in with the cooked bear meat and other ingredients, adding just a bit more wine if the mix is too dry. Just before serving, turn the heat off, stir in the sour cream, cover the pan, and let sit 5 minutes. Serves four.

8

Dressing Upland Birds and Waterfowl

As long as I live I will never forget the superb dove hunting Sam Piatt and I relished along Kentucky's banks of the Ohio River.

This is rich farm country, and without exception the prime bottomlands we hunt are planted with either corn or soybeans each year. There are just enough dead tree snags around the perimeters of the fields for us to hang our decoys, plus narrow fingers of vegetation to hide in and waylay birds trading back and forth between their feeding grounds and roosting sites.

However, it is the personality of September afternoons in northern Kentucky to be scorching hot, so we tote small camping coolers to our hunting locations where they serve triple duty. We can sit upon them when we are tired or when suspicious doves begin avoiding the obvious silhouettes of standing man-figures. The coolers also, of course, contain cold beverages which we gulp with rapid abandon when the mercury is hovering around the 95-degree mark. Finally, as we are sitting and sipping lemonade, patiently waiting for other birds to dive in, we bide our time cleaning the birds already killed. Then we wrap them in small plastic sandwich bags and bury them in crushed ice.

It is the rule, not the exception, for dinner guests to remark upon the succulent flavor of the doves we bag. Sometimes we broil them over hickory coals, other times they are slowly simmered in a cast-iron skillet along with thick brown gravy and served beside homemade biscuits.

Anyway, the ongoing argument we enjoy is that Sam usually contends the birds taste so good because of their steady diet of corn and soybeans. I beg to differ. I have eaten doves killed elsewhere by other

147

hunters – doves also grown plump on beans and corn – that were not nearly as tender and delicious. So I logically deduce the "something extra" resulting in our unusually tasty birds has to do with their being cleaned and drawn within minutes after being killed, and then immediately submitted to the coolers and the chilling effect of the cracked ice.

The thing that is significant here is that doves are not a case alone. Typically, I notice precisely the same results when hunting blue or spruce grouse in the western states, partridge on my farm in southern Ohio, quail in the Carolinas, ringneck pheasant in South Dakota, geese in Illinois and ducks along the eastern seaboard.

To be sure, nobody in his right mind would strap an ice chest on his back and then engage in the 10-mile hikes often required to collect a limit of chukars or ruffed grouse. Therefore, the only practical means of using such a cooler is when sitting in a blind of sorts. But hunters who have to hoof it long distances during the course of their outings can do nearly as well if they keep such a cooler in their hunting car or pickup truck, and plan their daily ramblings so that it is convenient to periodically return to where they have parked and secure their birds on ice. If it is not convenient, at least the iced-down cooler is there and waiting for the long drive home, and that is a far better state of affairs than allowing the game to barbecue in your coat pocket as you go tooling down the road.

Field Care of Feathered Game

As I have emphasized, I like to take a minute or two to field-dress fowl the instant it is in hand. I believe removing the innards of feathered game helps to cool the meat quickly and thereby prevents spoilage. Also, shot pellets may have penetrated the viscera and caused a leakage of digestive matter that may give birth to bacterial organisms and subsequently impart objectionable flavors.

There are several popular ways of field-dressing upland game-birds and waterfowl, depending upon their sizes. With small game such as quail, doves, timberdoodles, wood ducks or teal, use a small forked stick, or one of those pocketknives that has a bird-cleaning hook in place of one of the blades. Using either gadget, the stick or hook is carefully inserted into the bird's vent for several inches, slowly twisted to snare the entrails, and then withdrawn to clean the body cavity of all intestines and organs.

With medium-size gamebirds such as pheasants, grouse, chukars and most duck species, use the tip of your knife blade to enlarge the vent just slightly. Then either reach in with two fingers, pull the innards out and cut the lower intestine at the vent, or use a larger-size forked hook.

With large game such as wild turkey and geese, extend the cut made at the vent by a couple of inches, going in the direction of the breast bone, so that you may insert your entire hand to grasp the entrails.

When field-dressing any of the larger upland or waterfowl species, save the livers, hearts and gizzards, which can be used in the making of stuffing, gravies, stews and even gourmet spreads for sandwiches or crackers.

I then like to take a quantity of dry grass, ferns or moss and wipe the body cavity of the bird of any remaining fluids. Another idea, if one can remember (I usually can't), is to fold a number of paper towels and put them in your jacket pocket. One or two of the towels can be used to wipe out the bird, and another for cleaning your hands when the dressing operation is completed.

Bleeding upland gamebirds or waterfowl may be necessary, particularly the larger specimens, depending upon how much blood was in evidence when cleaning the body cavity. If there is not much, which usually is the case, simply cut across the large blood vessels in the neck region and hold the bird upside-down by the legs for a few minutes and what little blood remains will quickly drain away.

If the bird you have taken has a full crop (feel with your fingers for a seedy bulge in the lower gullet), carefully slice open the neck region with your knife and remove both the crop and esophagus. Once the thin neck skin is opened, you can easily peel these body parts away with your fingers and only minimal cutting.

Generally, it's also wise to check the condition of the preen gland. This double-lobed, buttonlike appendage located at the base of the tail contains an oily substance that avian creatures use to waterproof their feathers. If the preen gland has been punctured by shot pellets, or damaged in some other way (perhaps by a hard-mouthed retriever), it may be leaking its fluid, and any meat the oil comes in contact with will have a bitter taste. Otherwise, like the tarsal glands on deer legs, simply exercise caution not to disturb the gland and it should present no problem.

Now, with the head, feathers, feet and other body parts still intact, place the bird in a plastic bag of the appropriate size and then bury it in the ice near the top of your cooler (never at the very bottom where melt water will accumulate).

In those situations in which a cooler is not at the immediate kill site, use a well-ventilated game bag made of porous canvas or similar material. I consider this very important because in recent years hunters have been striving to improve their images by presenting dapper appearances, especially when contacting landowners for permission to hunt. They have been buying hunting jackets with game bags lined with rubber, plastic or nylon. The philosophy here is that such easily cleaned materials keep the hunter's garments from being permanently bloodstained. Very true. But such non-porous fabrics also cause the game to sweat by not allowing the circulation of air, and this, combined with the heat of other birds in the bag and the hunter's own body heat, can spell the ruination of game in less than an hour if the air temperature exceeds 70 degrees. Using these types of game bags, there have been occasions in which I've arrived home, removed my birds, and actually noticed them to be damp, as if they had been in a sauna or steam bath.

This is why I suggest hunters go back to their canvas game bags, and before securing birds in them to carefully field-dress the game, bleed it, and wipe the body cavity of any fluids, to virtually eliminate any fabric staining whatever. Should you notice a few blood spots or other stains when you arrive home, do not delay. Immediately soak the fabric in cold water and scrub it with a stiff bristle brush and it should come clean (this chore is easily facilitated if you've planned ahead and purchased your hunting jacket with a removable game bag).

How do you transport from the field the livers, hearts and gizzards you've saved? I usually like to place them in an empty bread wrapper to keep them clean, then merely secure them in the game bag with the birds.

With small gamebirds such as quail and woodcock, an alternative to a game bag is one of those special belt-hangers made for this purpose. These consist either of leather thongs with lengthwise slits near their ends, or pear-shaped wire holders that always remind me of shower curtain rings. In either case, they go around the necks of birds to hold them in place around your waist so that the game is continually exposed to fresh breezes. However, despite magazine pictures you may have seen, such devices aren't at all suitable for larger birds such as pheasants or grouse. The game flops around too much, which is an added hindrance no one needs when trying to push through dense brush cover or to cat-claw his way up a steep, alder-infested hillside.

When hunting waterfowl from a blind, lay your field-dressed ducks or geese on their backs in a shaded, breezy location, with a small stick spreading the lower abdomen walls to speed cooling.

A cooler filled with ice is usually sufficient for transporting birds home if less than three or four days' travel time is involved. If a much longer journey is required, better play it safe and use dry ice. Advance preparation for this requires nothing more than stowing in your car trunk a wooden box or styrofoam camping cooler filled with sawdust or shredded newspaper. The dry ice itself is very inexpensive and can be obtained from any dairy or ice cream plant near where you are hunting. (For more details concerning the proper use of dry ice, see Chapter 1).

Skinning or Plucking?

Many hunters favor the quick and easy way of peeling off the breast skin of small birds, such as doves, quail, woodcock or some of the diminuitive duck species, and then merely pulling out the breast and discarding the rest. Sometimes they even like to skin larger birds in a similar manner. Yet traditionalists are aghast at such behavior and look upon it as being as disreputable as potting birds on the ground. This school, given the slightest opportunity, will utter reprimands, insisting the only "honorable" way is plucking each and every bird, no matter what the species or its size.

I say there is no advantage in being a conformist to any school of thought. Decide what to do based upon the age and condition of the birds in question, the time you have available, what you, rather than someone else, enjoy most, the type of recipe you plan to use, and any other factors that seem pertinent at the time.

Generally, I like to pluck larger gamebirds, such as grouse and pheasant, whenever I am lucky enough to bag juveniles, and I usually

1. **1.** Many hunters disagree with the popular idea of plucking turkeys – and skin them instead, claiming excellent results. Here, a hunter begins by cutting off the lower legs. *Photo courtesy of Steve Price*

2. **2.** The next step is to carefully slit open the breast skin and begin peeling it back across the breast. *Photo courtesy of Steve Price*

3. **3.** Continue pulling the skin (with feathers still attached) all the way around the sides of the bird and across the back, then down the legs. Last, cut off the head and trim away loose remnants of skin. *Photo courtesy of Steve Price*

pluck somewhat smaller birds, such as quail, regardless of their ages. Young ducks are plucked as well, and all geese, because I invariably broil or roast these birds and like the skin intact for a more pleasing appearance. But if part of the body is badly shot up, and some of the meat unsalvageable, I peel off the breast skin, cut the breast out, and plan on a recipe calling for braising or perhaps a casserole.

Other birds that are unusually small—doves, for example—are an entirely different matter, as they contain so little meat on the legs and wings that plucking the entire bird adds up to a monumental waste of time. The same applies to diving ducks.

In deciding whether to skin or pluck, take into account some other things as well. The unique flavors of feathered game are found mostly in the skin, or in the thin layer of fat lying directly underneath. So naturally, you'll want to retain the skin on those birds that sometimes are otherwise a bit bland, such as ringnecks and bobwhites. But you'll probably want to remove the distasteful-flavored skin from fish-eating game such as gallinules and coots (also called scoters or mudhens). The age of the bird is important, too. As I will describe later, young birds should probably be broiled or roasted (for this you'll want the skin left on to retain moisture), while older birds become tough and dry when prepared by those methods. For them, pan-braising, oven-braising, or use in soups or stews is better, and these slow-cooking techniques enjoy no special benefit when the skin is left on.

To breast out small gamebirds such as doves you don't even need a knife. Using your hands alone, hold the carcass securely in your left hand and use your right hand to twist off one wing and then the other. They will snap off cleanly at the joint. Then jab your thumb into the body cavity beneath the breast bone, lift it up and away, and then with a gentle snap of your wrist separate it from the rest of the body. For somewhat larger birds such as quail or small waterfowl species, you can use the same technique, but heavy-duty scissors, shears or light-weight tin snips may come in handy for severing the wing joints and shoulder-to-back attachments.

Plucking takes more time but is worth the effort with larger game-birds that have seen minimum pellet damage, with most all waterfowl species except the small diving ducks and, as I have said before, with all birds that are to be roasted or broiled.

The feathers come away easiest when the birds are still warm, but often it is quite inconvenient to pluck birds in the field or blind.

In plucking birds, it's generally best to grab pinches of feathers in your fingers and pull them in the direction they grow. Plucking is easiest when done as soon as possible after the game has been killed.

This means later when you are home the feathers will seem more securely attached.

I have seen many hunters begin their plucking operations by promptly cutting off the tails, heads and feet of their game. If that's what you like, fine and dandy. I like to reserve these steps until the very last. Both upland gamebirds and waterfowl are sometimes a bit awkward to work with, and feet and other appendages offer convenient "handles."

From my experience, plucking is easiest by merely using the thumb and forefinger to pick out clumps of feathers; avoid tearing the skin by plucking the feathers downward in the direction they grow. It is futile to try to remove each and every feather by hand. With young birds, for example, many pin feathers will remain and they are best extracted, one by one, with tweezers; better still, contact a doctor or nurse and obtain a pair of no longer used surgical forceps or a Kelly clamp. A lot of tiny down feathers and fuzz may also remain on the body and these are best singed off. Do this as the very last step by quickly passing the body back and forth over the open flame of a gas range burner. If you don't have a gas range, or prefer not to do the work in your kitchen, use Sterno Canned Heat. This is an inexpensive type of jellied alcohol, available in any sporting-goods store, and a six-ounce can should last several years.

There are many types of commercial gizmos on the market for mechanically picking birds. To my knowledge, all of them operate on the same basic principle and have some type of drum or cylinder possessing dozens of little rubber fingers or several large flaps of rubber sheeting material. The drum rotates fast and accomplishes feather removal in almost no time at all without tearing the skin. Companies that make these mechanical pickers originally intended them for farmers and poultry growers to use in plucking domestic chickens, turkeys, ducks and geese, but since they are so efficient it was predictable that hunters would quickly pick up on the idea to make life a little easier when faced with the chore of plucking upland gamebirds and waterfowl.

The least expensive pickers, for sportsmen who kill perhaps less than 25 birds in any given year, are those made by the McKendree Products Company, 1893 Del Moro, Klamath Falls, Oregon 97601. Both their duck picker and chicken picker (suitable also for gamebirds) look basically the same and cost around $25. The drums containing the rubber fingers or blades are mounted on a spindle which can be secured in the chuck of any electric drill in the same way you'd install a drill bit. Then the drill is mounted sideways on some type of flat working surface such as a table top or workbench. You can invent your own mounting device, using clamps or blocks of wood with thumb screws, or for a few bucks you can purchase in a hardware store a special drill-mounting frame. In either case, of course, the drill must have a button that locks the drill into continuous speed, so you don't have to keep your finger on the trigger. Then, merely hold the duck or pheasant against the whirling drum and watch the feathers fly.

For those who kill a large number of birds each year, as in the case of hunters who regularly visit shooting preserves where the hunting of pen-raised birds is permissable almost year-around, it's worth considering a much larger, professional-model bird picker.

These work on the same principle but consist of entirely self-

1. Several types of mechanical pluckers will fit in an electric drill chuck. Mount the drill on a work surface, turn it on, and the bird will be plucked clean in about two minutes.

2. Here is a good mechanical device for picking ducks and geese. Rubber fingers do the work. Most such gadgets cost around $20.

contained units with one-horsepower motors and larger drums with more rubber fingers. They're designed for permanent installation somewhere, so that one does not find himself constantly having to perform a facelift on his electric drill.

The devices we're describing here range in price from about $90 all the way up to $275. If that sounds like a lot of money (it is!), one way of paring down the expense is for several regular hunting partners to jointly buy one of the machines and install it in one of their garages. Or, why not suggest at your next hunting or shooting club meeting that a professional bird picker be bought with club funds? In this manner, with the machine installed somewhere on the club's premises, hunters can stop at the club on the way home from an outing to clean their game. Anyway, it's the best excuse I've ever come up with for having a cold beer with the boys, while at the same time dressing my birds and subtly trying to get others to divulge where they are finding their woodcock, or ruffed grouse, or blue-winged teal.

One reason for the wide price spread on some of the professional pickers described above is the variety of optional accessories that can be purchased. One model, for example, has an attached blower fan and a large re-usable bag that clamps onto the blower's mouth assembly. The advantage of this is that when the picker is in operation, all of the feathers that fly from the carcass are instantly sucked into the bag, which keeps the work surface clean and allows easy disposal of the feathers. Two manufacturers of such equipment that I can highly recommend are the Magna American Corporation, P.O. Box 90, Raymond, Mississippi 39154, and the Pickwick Company, 1120 Glass Road N.E., Cedar Rapids, Iowa 52402.

Up to this point, we've been looking at dry picking and plucking methods. But sometimes dry plucking can be virtually impossible.

Expensive, but worthwhile if several buddies chip in, is a commercial duck picker. This one costs $220 and features a special blower and collection bag to gather feathers as they are quickly stripped away.

The feathers are too securely attached, and yanking too hard on them only serves to tear the skin. This is often what happens with certain species of ducks, geese and wild turkeys, and nearly all older game-birds.

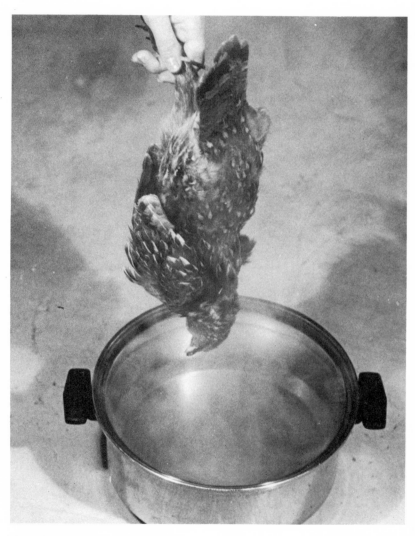

When feathers seem too firmly attached to gamebirds, they can be loosened by dunking the bird briefly in scalding water. Then pluck as usual and the feathers should come away quickly.

The easiest solution is to hold the bird by the feet and dunk the entire carcass into scalding hot water for a few seconds. But a word of caution: make sure the water is no hotter than 180 degrees, and dunk the bird only briefly, or you may parboil the meat and cause the skin to slip. All that's necessary is to dunk the bird, slosh it up and down a bit so the hot water reaches underneath the feathers to where they are attached to their follicles, then pull the bird out and try to wet pluck the feathers. They should now come away easily, either by hand or when contacted by the rubber fingers or blades of a mechanical picker, but if they are still securely attached you can always make a second, very brief dunking.

Another method, one that is quite popular with duck and goose hunters, is the wax-dunking method Fill a large, deep pail with water, but not so high that it will overflow when the duck or goose is submerged. Heat it to about 180 degrees (never to the boiling point, which is 212 degrees). Then add five or six blocks of paraffin of the type used for canning jellies and jams. They're available in any grocery store. You can also purchase special Duck Wax from the Pickwick Company mentioned earlier, and Cabela's, 812 13th Avenue, Sidney, Nebraska 69162, sells what they call Super Duxwax in 10-pound blocks.

Either of these two commercial products, or simple paraffin from your local supermarket, melts when added to the pail of hot water and should float to the top in a layer 1½ to 2 inches thick. Then holding the duck or goose by the feet, dip it into the bucket, slosh it around for just a few seconds and quickly remove the bird. Next, hang the bird by the feet until the paraffin has completely cooled and congealed. Then, pull the wax away with your fingers, just like peeling the shell from a hardboiled egg, and along with the wax will come nearly all of the feathers. As a final step it probably will be necessary to pat the carcass dry with paper towels and then pick out a few remaining pin feathers or primaries on the wings.

As I am peeling away the wax I like to drop the pieces with the imbedded feathers right back into the bucket. When I am done, I can fish globs of feathers out with a forked stick, allow the water to cool and the wax to solidify, then pry out the chunk of wax and use it over again and again.

One word of caution: some types of waxes and paraffins are highly flammable, so good advice is to use them outdoors.

After the feathers have been entirely removed, the next step is to cut off the head, feet, tail and in some cases the wingtips. Then either disjoint the bird, quarter it or halve it just like you would a chicken, or wrap the bird whole for freezing if you don't have plans to eat it within the next few days.

Another trick is worth noting but it involves telling a brief story about an outdoor-writer friend of mine by the name of Harrison Williams. Several years ago he wrote a magazine article about preparing gamebirds for the table and the story was accompanied by a number of step-by-step photos that Harrison claimed, in the story, were of spruce grouse. To me, they looked like regular barnyard chickens as they sat all nicely dressed on a roasting pan destined for the oven.

The next time I saw Williams I began some friendly ribbing about how he was such a lousy wingshot that he just couldn't kill any grouse in time to make his magazine deadline and so had to resort to the use of chickens for his pictures, hoping readers wouldn't be able to tell the difference.

"Nope," Williams swore with his hand raised, "those were spruce grouse all right."

"Couldn't have been," I joked. "They were too plump and perfect looking, not like any gamebirds I've ever killed."

That is when—I suppose Williams told me this more to save face than anything else—he divulged a little-known secret.

Dunking upland gamebirds or waterfowl into hot wax or water has a tendency to shrink the skin and make the birds look skinny. Poultry growers remedy the problem by soaking their plucked birds in ice water. This gives a plump appearance far more pleasing for the table.

"My uncle owns a chicken ranch in New Mexico," he confided, "and a long time ago I worked for him one summer. He'd scald his birds before picking them but the birds, after being in the hot water, always came out looking kind of scrawny and unshapely. Well, to make for the most pleasing appearance, so his customers would be happy, Unc then did something else. After all his chickens were plucked, he'd then dunk them in a big tank of ice water. He left them in the ice water for one hour, then pulled them out, and you wouldn't believe the change and how big and plump they now looked."

As it happened, Harrison Williams tried the same ruse with his gamebirds and the results were identical. As he explained, the hot water causes shrinkage. The ice water reverses this, causing the bird carcasses not only to return to their former shapes but actually to absorb moisture and swell up slightly. The cold water also improves the keeping qualities and tenderness of almost all fowl species. Although one hour is plenty long enough for medium-size birds such as grouse and pheasants, 30 minutes is usually sufficient for quail and other smaller species. By the same token, large ducks, geese and wild turkeys should be left in the ice water for 18 to 24 hours for thorough chilling to take place.

Not surprisingly, I've since learned that commercial poultry companies now are also largely using this technique in which tens of thousands of chickens, Rock Cornish hens, turkeys and similar domestic species are routinely sent through both hot- and cold-water baths.

Aging Upland Gamebirds and Waterfowl

Aging is a process whereby feathered game is allowed to hang for a prescribed length of time to allow the effects of deterioration to begin to set in. Although this breakdown of the muscle fibers causes the meat to be more tender than otherwise, it also yields a stronger flavor.

For generations, Europeans have insisted upon aging their upland gamebirds and waterfowl – and what's more, with the innards intact! They hang their birds in a cool, dry location for as long as 14 days, or until such time as the tail feathers begin to fall away. Perhaps their tastebuds are more developed than mine, because in order to keep from losing my breakfast I must respectfully stand upwind of such aging birds.

On this side of the Atlantic, upland hunters and waterfowlers often like to age their game as well, but seldom to such extremes. They first eviscerate their birds, and then hang them with heads, feathers and other body parts intact for two or three days at most. I can heartily recommend this if you like a particular species of feathered game to have a slightly more tangy, outdoorsy flavor than it ordinarily presents.

The best aging temperature is about 38 degrees, and the best location is shaded, dry, slightly breezy and protected from pets. Those birds in which most of the shot contacted the upper body regions (head, breast, wings) should be hung by the feet. Those with lower body wounds (abdomen, back, tail) should be hung by the head. This facilitates drainage of remaining body fluids without their needlessly passing over or through other parts of the anatomy. Use any type of cord or twine you have on hand to hang the birds, spaced at least a foot apart so they are not allowed to touch each other.

Another way to accomplish the aging effect of tenderizing birds and giving them more flavor, but with absolutely no risk of spoilage, is by placing them in the lower compartment of your refrigerator for several days. This is an especially wise practice in warm climates. In this case it's usually best to pluck your birds first, then place the carcasses inside plastic bags; otherwise, picking the chilled birds may be very difficult.

Although it is a much slower process, freezing upland gamebirds and waterfowl for several months also sees the gradual breakdown in the cells in connective tissue for more tender eating but little change in flavor.

9

Duck and Goose Delights

When it comes to outdoor adventures, my friend Jim Beming believes nothing takes a back seat to waterfowl hunting, especially if it is in the company of a faithful retriever.

But it is after several ducks or a prime goose are in the bag, Beming contends, that the real fun begins. You see, in addition to being an ardent marsh hunter, a gunstock maker by trade, and a skilled dog trainer, Jim considers himself quite an accomplished wild-game chef. Few things in life give him greater pleasure than experimenting with waterfowl recipes and then bestowing their distinctive flavors upon eager guests crowding the dining room.

"There is much more to the rich tradition of preparing waterfowl for the table than merely plopping a bird into the oven for a prescribed length of time," Beming recently explained when I was looking over his shoulder in the kitchen of an old and highly respected gunning club near Chesapeake Bay. "First, you have to have the right attitude. Do you know why the vast majority of famous chefs are always men? It's because of their attitude. You see, the way our society has evolved, cooking has often been looked upon as a burden to be carried by women. Hence, in a great many cases women cook only because they feel they have to. Men, on the other hand, generally are not put in the position of feeling they *have* to cook. So when they do cook it's almost always because cooking gives them pleasure. Because they love it. And that frame of mind is far more important to the outcome of any meal than any recipe ever invented.

"But about cooking waterfowl, one thing you'll want to do at the outset," Beming continued, "is determine the age of the bird, as that plays a crucial role in deciding whether to broil, roast, braise or stew-cook your fowl. With ducks, even the species should be taken into account, and an appropriate recipe used, because the diets of different birds vary and this in turn affects their flavors."

How Old is Your Bird?

Geese, whatever the species, may live as long as 20 years. All make for outstanding table fare with their lean, dark meat if the lucky hunter has first guessed his bird to be young, middle-aged or an old codger. Often this is easy to do before the goose even hits the ground because geese typically organize their flying regiments by age. The older veterans take the lead, middle-aged birds follow, and the young of the year bring up the rear. Consequently, many hunters like to pass up shooting opportunities at the front-flyers, knowing those trailing behind will be more tender.

This tactic only applies to gunning flight birds. When individuals are barreling into shooting range in cornfields, or a hunter is pass-shooting at birds heading for their evening resting sites, there is no alternative but to take the shots awarded and try to accurately age the birds later.

Generally, older geese can be identified by their coarser, thicker plumage and rounded or pointed tail-feather tips. Also, the breast skin when rubbed between thumb and forefinger seems a bit leathery. Juvenile and middle-aged birds, on the other hand, are loaded with pin feathers; their tail feathers are likely to show a V-shaped notch, and the breast skin seems soft and pliable.

Determining the age of ducks is done along the same lines but is far less critical. Since they seldom live more than a few years, the chances are far greater the hunter will bag young and therefore tender birds. Yet in the cases of either ducks or geese, don't make the easy mistake of judging a bird's age by its size alone. Sometimes the rule holds true, but there are plenty of nonconformists flying around that never read the book and are larger or smaller than average for their ages.

Which Species Provide Best Table Fare?

Waterfowl that has fed upon wild rice, celery, similar aquatic foods and domestic grains such as corn and wheat are far superior in flavor to others such as mergansers that forsake strict vegetarian diets and become fish-eaters, or dine occasionally upon other animal forms such as snails, leeches, tadpoles and the like.

As a result, in the duck category canvasbacks and redheads are universally looked upon as providing the best eating, followed by mallards, black ducks, wigeons, pintails and the three species of teal (blue-winged, green-winged and cinnamon). Teal invariably average only 12 ounces in weight, while the others may go anywhere from 2 to 3 pounds.

Of the geese, the Canadas are best known. There are 11 subspecies of the Canada, ranging from cackling Canadas of only 2½ pounds in weight to giant Canadas that may tip the scales at better than 20 pounds. Probably the average Canada most hunters collect comes in around 8 or 10 pounds. Blue, brant, white-fronted and lesser snow geese ranging in size from 4 to 12 pounds also are sure to please all dinner guests.

Advance Preparations

If we go back to basics, proper field care of waterfowl significantly influences later taste tests. This means removing the bird's insides as quickly as possible and then allowing the body temperature to rapidly undergo further chilling by any of several means. A jumbo camping cooler filled with crushed ice is one effective idea (place your birds in large plastic bags near the top of the cooler, so they don't soak in melt water). At other times Mother Nature may provide the necessary refrigeration by means of cool breezes. Duck hunting, in fact, is often characterized by such driving winds, sleet and horrendously cold air temperatures that it is not unknown for hunters to abandon their blinds and partake of any number of indoor sports.

However, aside from cooling their duck or goose carcasses, many hunters like to enact other culinary strategies just prior to cooking. It has been my experience that the strong, gamey flavors claimed of some waterfowl usually are more imagined than real (coots, gallinules and similar shorebirds are notable exceptions). Nevertheless, if a hunter has diagnosed his duck or goose as likely being an older bird, or suspects it may have an objectionable flavor due to feeding upon certain organic matter, here are two suggestions.

In the case of older birds, soak them overnight in a brine solution. I use a deep plastic bowl for most ducks, but a large plastic pail is necessary for geese, to ensure the fowl are completely covered with the salty liquid. To make the brine, prepare a mixture of two tablespoons salt, one tablespoon vinegar and one quart water (proportionately increase these amounts if a greater quantity of brine is required). If you do not care for the very subtle flavor the vinegar imparts, Jim Beming suggests substituting one tablespoon of baking soda instead. Next, cover the bowl with a lid or sheet of aluminum foil and place the works in the lower compartment of your refrigerator. The following day, completely rinse the bird with fresh, cold water and then pat the carcass dry with paper toweling before trying your favorite recipe.

If a bird is suspected to be overly strong in flavor, it's best to go one step further. After the bird has undergone the overnight brine soaking, place it back in the refrigerator for another night, this time with several slices of celery and onion in the body cavity. These vegetables will absorb strong flavors and aromas and at the same time impart to the meat their own subtle, pleasant flavors. To prevent the bird from drying out during this overnight refrigeration period, set it on a large plate or platter and cover completely with a damp cloth. The following morning, remove and discard the celery and onion slices.

Cooking Methods

Most experienced waterfowl cooks agree that roasting is the best way to prepare ducks. But wild ducks, unlike their fatty domesticated cousins, possess very lean meat and this means the longer a duck is cooked, the tougher it becomes. So there seems to be a consensus that, when roasted, all species of ducks should be served when they are crispy on the outside, medium-rare and juicy inside. Achieving this is no more mysterious than using a combination of very high oven heat and a short cooking time.

A good indication your roasting ducks are finished and ready for

More hunters should try making waterfowl stews. They are a simple, yet elegant way to enjoy the distinct flavors of various species when other cooking methods, such as roasting or broiling, would be inappropriate due to the age of the fowl.

the table is to wiggle the legs back and forth to see if they move easily. If not, leave the ducks in the oven for another five minutes and then try again.

Young ducks cut up into serving-size pieces can also be broiled in the same manner as chickens. But ducks suspected to be old should not be roasted or broiled as they will come out tough and dry. Instead, it is necessary to braise them, which is a slow-cooking method that adds moisture to the meat.

It should be mentioned that there is so little meat on the wings, drumsticks and backs of ducks that many hunters like to merely fillet out the breasts and thighs and cook them alone as their main dinner entrees. These can be roasted, broiled or braised, according to your preference and the ages of the birds. What meat remains on the carcass is very carefully separated from the bones, placed in the freezer and, when enough accumulates made, into a casserole, soup or stew.

Some hunters even use entire ducks, if they are older, for recipes such as stews. Occasionally it may be wise to use a younger bird, too, if it has been too severely damaged by shot to appear presentable by other cooking methods.

When figuring serving portions for recipes in which whole ducks are roasted, broiled or braised, any of the larger species averaging 2 to 2½ pounds should each feed two people. When preparing small ducks such as teal, allow one bird per person.

Due to their large sizes, young geese are usually roasted and, like ducks, should be cooked only until they are medium-rare. Older geese may be tough and stringy if roasted and so a better method for them is oven-braising. With either the roasting or braising method, again begin wiggling the legs about two-thirds of the way through the allotted cooking time to test for doneness.

Since the breast alone from an average-size goose will easily feed four hungry diners, many chefs prefer to roast the entire goose for the sake of appearance, but then serve only the breast meat, sliced very thinly across the grain. The less tender meat remaining on the legs and thighs is reserved for stews or soups.

Favorite Duck and Goose Recipes

Duck and goose hunting has a long and revered heritage in North

America and undoubtedly more recipes therefore exist for waterfowl than for any other type of game species found in the New World.

Following are a number of time-tested ideas that have gained special popularity over the years.

Jim Beming's Roasted Duck Breasts
6 duck breasts
½ cup flour
½ teaspoon salt
¼ teaspoon black pepper
6 tablespoons cooking oil
2 medium onions, chopped
1 cup chopped celery
3 teaspoons poultry seasoning
2 cups water
2 packages prepared, unseasoned stuffing mix

Fillet out the breasts of the ducks. Mix together the flour, salt and pepper and dredge the breasts until they are well dusted. Next, brown the breasts in a skillet containing the cooking oil. In a separate pan, sauté the onions and celery in just a tiny bit of cooking oil until they are tender and clear. Add the 2 cups of water and stir in the poultry seasoning. Then add the stuffing mix and stir thoroughly. Spread the stuffing mix on the bottom of a lightly greased roasting pan and arrange the browned duck breasts on top of the stuffing. Cover with a lid and roast for 1 hour in an oven pre-heated to 350 degrees. Serves four.

Remington Mallards
2 whole mallards, plucked
2 tablespoons cooking sherry
1 teaspoon celery salt
1 teaspoon celery seed
1 teaspoon onion salt
½ teaspoon curry powder
2 teaspoons salt
½ teaspoon black pepper
1 small onion, chopped
1 stalk celery, chopped

When history is written, chef Kelsor Smith's recipe from Remington Farms in Maryland will go down in the annals as having no equal. Place the ducks in a roasting pan breast up and sprinkle each with 1 tablespoon of the sherry. Then thoroughly mix all the remaining seasonings and spices and season each bird (use just a medium sprinkling; you may not want to use the entire quantity of seasoning mix). Next, distribute the chopped onion and celery in the pan around the birds. Now add about ½ inch of water to the pan. Bake at 500 degrees until the breasts are brown (about 20 minutes), then carefully turn the birds over and continue roasting until the backs are brown. Next, turn the birds over again so they are breast-side up, cover the roasting pan with a high lid and continue to cook 1 additional hour at 300 degrees. Serves four.

Chesapeake Barbecued Duck
2 whole ducks, plucked
½ pound butter or margarine
½ cup ketchup
1 tablespoon sugar
1½ tablespoons lemon juice
1 tablespoon Worcestershire Sauce
½ teaspoon black pepper
1 teaspoon salt
1 clove garlic, pressed
1 small onion, chopped
½ teaspoon Tabasco sauce

The Marlin Firearms Company offers this superb recipe for very special occasions. Split the two ducks in half lengthwise. Then slightly flatten the four halves with a wooden meat mallet or the broad side of a cleaver. Make the barbecue sauce by thoroughly mixing all the remaining ingredients and simmering them in a covered saucepan for 5 minutes. Place the duck halves in a roasting pan and then in an oven pre-heated to 375 degrees for about 50 minutes, basting them with the barbecue sauce every 10 minutes. After the allotted cooking time, carefully turn the ducks over and bake another 50 minutes, again basting every 10 minutes. (If you're in a hurry, or find you are missing some of the required ingredients, you can substitute 2 cups of Open Pit regular-style barbecue sauce). Serves four.

Broiled Duck
2 whole ducks, plucked
½ cup butter

Either split the ducks in half lengthwise or disjoint them into individual pieces. Any species is suitable as long as they are young birds. Place on a broiler pan and broil 10 minutes, basting twice with butter. Then turn the birds over and broil 10 minutes on the other side, again basting twice. Serves four.

Broiled Duck Extravaganza
2 whole ducks, plucked
¼ cup honey
3 tablespoons soy sauce
¼ cup sherry
1 clove garlic, crushed
½ teaspoon ginger

Split the ducks in half lengthwise and arrange on a broiler pan. Mix the remaining ingredients and heat gently in a saucepan for 3 minutes. Broil the ducks 10 minutes, basting twice with the sauce. Turn the ducks and broil another 10 minutes, again basting twice. Serves four.

Broiled Teal
4 whole teal, plucked (any species)
9 tablespoons butter
3 teaspoons lemon juice
¾ teaspoon black pepper

Split the birds in half lengthwise and arrange on a broiler pan. Combine the remaining ingredients in a saucepan and heat gently for 3 minutes. Broil the teal 10 minutes, basting twice. Then turn the birds and broil another 10 minutes, again basting twice. Serves four.

Braised Duck
2 ducks, cut into serving-size pieces
flour
cooking oil
water (or 2 cans chicken consommé)

Dredge individual breasts, drumsticks, thighs and so on with the flour and then brown them on all sides in a cast-iron skillet containing hot cooking oil, lard or bacon fat. Add several cups of water or chicken consommé, to come halfway up the sides of the duck pieces. Cover the pan with a lid, turn the heat down low, and let the ducks slowly bubble to perfection for 1 hour. Serves four.

Baked Duck L'Orange
2 whole ducks, plucked
2 Brown-in-Bags
2 tablespoons flour
¼ cup butter, melted
salt
1 apple, chopped
1 stalk celery, chopped
2 cups orange juice

Pre-heat your oven to 350 degrees. Shake 1 tablespoon flour in each Brown-in-Bag, and set them side by side in a deep roasting pan. Pour 1 cup orange juice into the bottom of each bag and stir to mix with the flour. Brush the outside of each duck with the butter, then lightly salt the outside and inside of each bird. Fill the body cavities of the two birds with the apple and celery. Place the birds in the bags, close the openings and make 6 half-inch slits in the top of each bag. Bake for 1½ hours. Serves four.

Wild Duck Supreme
2 whole ducks, plucked
½ teaspoon rosemary leaves
1 medium onion, cut into large chunks
1 apple, cut into chunks
2 stalks celery, chopped
½ cup butter or margarine, melted
1 teaspoon salt
1 teaspoon pepper

Mix together the salt, ½ teaspoon of the pepper and ¼ teaspoon of the rosemary leaves. Rub this mixture inside the body cavity and outside each duck. Place equal quantities of the apple, onion and celery in each body cavity, then place the ducks breast-side down on a wire rack in a shallow roasting pan. Roast for 40 minutes in an oven pre-heated to 350 degrees. Meanwhile, combine the butter, ½ teaspoon of the pepper and ¼ teaspoon of the rosemary leaves and begin basting the ducks every 10 minutes. After the allotted 40 minutes of roasting time, carefully turn the ducks so they are now breast-side up. Roast 50 minutes longer, basting every 10 minutes. Just before placing the ducks on a serving platter, remove and discard the apple and vegetables. Serves four.

Hunter's Duck

2 whole ducks, plucked
1 can chicken consommé (or 1 cup chicken bouillon)
½ cup sherry
bacon fat
2 stalks celery, chopped
1 large apple, chopped
1 medium onion, chopped
3 green onions (scallions), chopped
½ teaspoon parsley flakes
½ cup water chestnuts
1 cup mushroom caps
salt
pepper

Rub the body cavity of each duck with cool bacon fat, then lightly sprinkle with salt and pepper. Fill each body cavity with equal quantities of the chopped celery, apple and onion. Place the ducks in a deep roasting pan and fill with 2 inches of water to which has been added ¼ cup of the sherry and half the can of consommé. Bake at 300 degrees until half of the liquid has evaporated (about 40 minutes). Add the consommé and sherry you have left and continue cooking until the ducks are tender (about another 30 minutes). Remove the ducks from the pan and place where they will stay warm. Add to the roasting pan the green onions, mushrooms and water chestnuts (these can be obtained in the oriental foods section of your grocery store) and gently simmer until the onions are cooked. Meanwhile, carefully split the ducks in half lengthwise and place on a hot serving platter. Pour the vegetable medley sauce over the top of the ducks, sprinkle with the parsley flakes and serve. Serves four.

Holiday Duck

2 whole ducks, plucked
1 large onion, sliced in half
½ cup red wine
2 tablespoons butter
1 teaspoon thyme
salt
pepper

Line the bottom of a deep roasting pan with a large sheet of heavy duty aluminum foil that comes up well over the sides. Rub the inside of each duck with a bit of salt and pepper. Next, place inside each body cavity half of the onion. Set the ducks on the foil in the roasting pan and pour ¼ cup red wine over the tops of each, then sprinkle each duck with ½ teaspoon thyme. On top of each duck place a large dollop (1 tablespoon) of butter. Then bring the foil up over the top of the ducks and pinch until tightly sealed. Bake at 300 degrees for 3 hours. Serves four.

Brandied Duck

2 ducks, cut into serving-size pieces
¼ cup brandy
2 cups red wine
2 stalks celery, chopped
2 carrots, chopped
1 onion, chopped
½ cup butter
3 teaspoons parsley flakes
1 teaspoon salt
½ teaspoon black pepper
¼ teaspoon marjoram
¼ teaspoon thyme
1 cup mushroom caps

Place all of the ingredients except the butter and mushrooms in a saucepan and heat gently for 5 minutes. This forms a marinade which should then be allowed to cool completely. Place the marinade and duck pieces (older ducks that may be tough are ideal) in a deep glass bowl and let sit for 3 hours. Remove the ducks and pat dry with paper toweling, then brown in a skillet containing the butter. Pour the marinade into the skillet, cover and simmer over low heat for 1 hour. Transfer the ducks to a hot serving platter. Then strain the marinade into a saucepan to remove the vegetables, heat the liquid gently and add just a bit of cornstarch to thicken into a sauce. Sauté the mushrooms in butter, then add them to the sauce. Pour the sauce over the ducks and serve. Serves four.

Big John's Duck Soup

2 pounds duck meat, separated from bones
9 cups water
1 large carrot, chopped
1 large onion, chopped
2 stalks celery, chopped
1 teaspoon salt
6 chicken bouillon cubes
8 ounces thin noodles

Use older ducks for this recipe, birds that are badly shot up, or leftover less tender meat pieces from drumsticks, wings, thighs and backs. Add all the ingredients except the noodles to a deep pot, cover and simmer slowly on low heat for 3 hours. Twenty minutes before the allotted cooking time is finished, add the noodles. (A slight variation of this recipe is to substitute shredded cabbage for the celery. Another variation is to use only 8 cups of water and add 1 cup of chopped tomatoes. Also remember that less tender goose parts can be substituted for the duck meat).

Braised Goose

Like older ducks, older geese should be braised to ensure the meat is tender and juicy. But unlike ducks, which can be on top of the stove in a skillet, the sizes of honkers requires that they be braised in the oven, using a deep roasting pan with a high-standing lid. Simply place the goose in the roasting pan, breast-side up, along with 2 cups hot water, then cover and cook at 325 degrees for 25 minutes per pound.

Roast Goose

The favorite way to cook young geese is to roast them, but the large quantity of fat and drippings that accumulates in the roasting pan often poses a minor problem. An easy remedy is to begin the cooking with the goose lying breast down in the roasting pan. After about 30 minutes of cooking time at 450 degrees, drain off all the grease that has rendered out, which will be the majority. Then turn the bird so the breast is now up and finish the roasting at 350 degrees for 25 minutes per pound (an 8-pound bird will therefore require about 3½ hours cooking time). Even though there is a lot of fat in geese, it still may be wise to occasionally baste the breast and upper legs with some of the grease to ensure a crispy finish. But if the breast seems to be browning too quickly during the first 2 hours of cooking time, you may want to drape a sheet of aluminum foil loosely over the top of the bird.

Waterfowl Stuffing

Any prepared chicken or turkey stuffing goes well with large ducks or geese that are roasted whole. Simply follow the directions on the stuffing package and then fill the body cavity in the usual manner, being careful not to pack the stuffing too tightly to allow for expansion. Then close the opening with a large needle and cotton string.

However, if you elect to follow a poultry-stuffing recipe from scratch, use slightly less sage than the recipe calls for as the rich, dark meat of waterfowl will impart a unique tang of its own.

Also, instead of a conventional bread stuffing, many hunters like to fill the body cavity with pre-cooked wild rice, or with quartered onions, apples and celery, which add a special flavor but are discarded when the bird is served. Or, use no stuffing at all. Instead, 1 hour before the goose is finished, or ½ hour before the duck is finished, fill the roasting pan with sauerkraut so it entirely surrounds the bird.

10

A Treasury of Upland Gamebird Memories

They say history repeats itself. So it is not surprising that dining upon gamebirds began long before man was civilized and yet now is considered one of his most civilized pleasures.

The degree of refinement with which such repasts are undertaken, however, depends largely upon the individual and the sophistication of his tastes.

Hemingway, as a ready example, firmly believed pheasant was not fit for consumption until it had hung in some cool and dry location for a bare minimum of a week, preferably longer, and had almost but not quite reached the spoiling point.

Rough-rider Teddy Roosevelt frequently dined upon wild turkey and other gamebird species but never until after the undressed birds, feathers still intact, had been permitted to dangle from his saddle for two days as he rode beneath the scorching sun of the arid Southwest.

And discriminating woodcock hunters in England have long believed the only fitting way to serve their long-billed quarry is with the head tucked under the wing and the entrails left inside the body; one alternative to this sees the entrails removed and then mashed with a breading into a paste that is reinserted into the body as a form of stuffing.

To be sure, modern American sportsmen are seldom inclined to go to these extremes and usually resort to more conventional means of gamebird preparation. There are probably as many revered recipes as there are bird hunters to savor them, but it should always be looked upon as a rare privilege to dine upon upland game and to introduce others to gamebirds that have been masterfully prepared for the table, especially if each bird is one you have dropped yourself. And the sharing of those birds which are particularly difficult to bag, such as wild turkey, is even more justifiable cause for celebration with your closest friends.

If there is one cardinal rule in preparing upland game, though, it must be never to camouflage or disguise the distinctive flavors of the various upland species. A second canon, having to do with the serving, is to ensure that you present the variously delicate personalities of certain gamebirds only to those who you can be sure will most fully appreciate each mouthful. Quail, pheasant and turkey go over remarkably well with newcomers to upland dining, while it is best to reserve your woodcock, grouse and dove dinners for sharing with those who are well acquainted with their singular flavors.

Another long-accepted standard is that truly eventful upland gamebird repasts begin not within the confines of your kitchen but in the field, the very moment your pattern of chilled shot has found its mark. So if the reader is one who finds himself prone to skipping around rather than reading book chapters in their due sequence, stop! Go back and read the previous sections having to do with field care of gamebirds, plucking and skinning, and aging (found in Chapter 8), as all of these are contributory ingredients at least as important, if not more so, than those of tins and jars.

The Best of the Best

Over the years I have tried hundreds of ways of preparing various gamebird species, and enjoy experimenting with new recipe ideas of my own. But when the chips are down and it's imperative that certain guests enjoy a memorable feed, the recipes that follow are the very special ones I rely upon without reservation. You can be confident they will please even the most discriminating tastebuds.

Plantation Quail

With dogs ranging wide and far we followed on horseback, occasionally dismounting to work a pointed covey. The plantation, not a large one, consisted of a white colonial house with front-porch pillars and a stable to the rear, situated on 480 acres of some of Georgia's finest bobwhite territory. After 15 birds had been killed, Mr. Jim, a lanky black keeper and trainer of the estate's dozen or so dogs, turned his steed and rode back to the kitchen.

We would continue to hunt for another two hours and then return for dinner, master-chef Ray Blunn meanwhile having prepared the birds in classical Southern style. Though I have dined upon quail often, I do not think I will ever forget that meal.

Ray believed in first plucking the birds and then singeing off the remaining down in order to conserve the extra bit of flavor and moisture the skin affords.

Then the birds were rubbed with flour, lightly salted and peppered, and slipped into a pan of bubbling butter until well browned on all sides. Next, Ray lowered the heat, added a bit of water, covered the pan and allowed the birds to simmer for 45 minutes. When tender they were removed to a warming plate, and gravy was made by adding flour to the drippings in the pan. When stirred smooth, a little milk was then added until the gravy was of just the right consistency.

The bobwhites were lusciously tender on the inside, yet golden brown on the breasts, and they were served two per person on toast with the gravy ladled over the top. Complementing the dish were fried hominy squares, applesauce and steaming mugs of strong black coffee.

Broiled Quail
whole quail (1 or 1½ per person)
flour
salt
pepper
melted butter

If the weather permits, quail are superb when broiled over a bed of hardwood chunks that have been allowed to reduce themselves to white-ash embers. Unlike other gamebirds, which may be hung and aged and even frozen after that, quail should be eaten as soon as possible after killing.

Split each whole quail in half lengthwise. Now rub a mixture of flour, salt and pepper into the skin, and then lay the birds upon any type of cooking grate that has been brushed with vegetable oil to prevent them from sticking. I like to position the grate only 3 inches above the coals to momentarily sear the birds on all sides. Then I raise the grate 6 to 8 inches higher for the remainder of the cooking until the birds are tender on the inside. During the broiling process, baste often with a brush and melted butter.

Quail are best when eaten soon after they have been killed. Here, bobwhites have been split lengthwise into halves and are broiling over a bed of hardwood coals.

When the birds are brown and done, serve two or three halves to each individual on buttered toast with a side portion of grape jelly. Any green vegetable of your choosing will go well with broiled quail and a fitting beverage is imported ale in pre-chilled pilsner glasses.

> *Quail with Mushrooms*
> 8 quail
> 8 strips bacon
> 1 cup butter, melted
> 30 button mushrooms
> juice from ½ lemon

For a special evening dinner menu, Quail with Mushrooms is without peer. Truss each bird with a strip of bacon held in place with a toothpick and then lay them in a large buttered roasting pan. Next place the birds in an oven pre-heated to 350 degrees for ½ hour. Meanwhile, in another pan on top of your stove, sauté whole button mushrooms in ½ cup melted butter until they are done; you'll need about 30 mushrooms, and when they are finished set them aside on a warming plate.

Just as the quail are almost done, remove the bacon strips from them. Add ½ cup more butter to that remaining in the pan the mushrooms sautéed in, and when it is fully melted use it to baste the quail. Now turn the oven up to 375 degrees for a few minutes until the breasts and upper legs of the birds are brown and crispy.

Remove the birds to a warming plate and add just a bit of water and the juice from half a lemon to the drippings in the bottom of the roasting pan and stir continuously to make a gravy. The quail and mushrooms can now be served side by side with the gravy ladled over the top. Any vegetable goes well with this special meal, but I especially recommend glazed carrots and several spoonfuls per person of currant jelly. Serves four.

> *Partridge Supreme*
> 4 partridge breasts
> 2 cans condensed mushroom soup
> 1 small onion, diced
> flour
> melted butter
> salt

Ruffed grouse which have fed upon beechnuts, or perhaps wild grapes, rank in culinary excellence far above birds that have foraged upon sumac or greenbrier. But with this particular recipe, birds that have fed upon almost anything will afford dining pleasures of exceptionally high caliber.

Of the many grouse species, the author rates ruffed grouse as the best eating. And of many favorite recipes, Partridge Supreme is his favorite.

In preparing Partridge Supreme only the breasts are used (save the legs and at some other date fry them up like chicken) and should be separated carefully from the remainder of the body and not split in half.

Dust the breasts with flour and then brown them on all sides (about 5 minutes) in a frying pan containing melted butter. Remove the breasts from the skillet, drain and sprinkle lightly with salt. Now place the breasts in a deep, oven-tempered glass casserole dish. Pour on top of the breasts 2 cans of condensed cream of mushroom soup (or cream of celery soup), sprinkle with a small diced onion, cover with a loose-fitting lid and bake in a pre-heated 350 degree oven for exactly 70 minutes.

When ready to serve, generously ladle spoonfuls of the mushroom or celery gravy from the bottom of the casserole dish over the breasts.

It is imperative that grouse prepared in this manner be served as the sole feature of a dinner with little in the way of side dishes detracting from the main emphasis. The only accompaniments I would suggest with this meal might be tender young mushrooms that have been sautéed in lightly seasoned butter and several tablespoons per person of a mixture of wild and white rice. Serves four.

Partridge Breasts Stroganoff
2 partridge breasts
2 tablespoons butter, melted
1 onion, finely diced
¾ cup sliced mushrooms
1 teaspoon basil
¾ cup sour cream
salt
pepper

A meal fit for dukes and earls, Partridge Breasts Stroganoff is absolutely perfect for late-night dinners. Begin by sautéeing in 2 tablespoons of butter a finely diced onion until it is clear. Remove the onion and reserve for later, now placing two partridge breasts in the same pan and adding just a bit more butter. Cover and cook gently on low heat until the breasts are tender (about 45 minutes), then transfer them to an oven set on low heat to keep them warm.

Still using the same pan, brown the sliced mushrooms, adding a sprinkling of salt and pepper and 1 teaspoon basil. Then stir in the sour cream and the cooked onion and next add the partridge breasts. Cover and simmer for 15 minutes. Remove the breasts from the pan and serve on toast, spooning the gravy from the pan over the tops of the breasts.

Very tender, small green peas or baby limas go well with this dish, and you may also like long-grain wild rice. Serves two.

Roast Grouse
whole ruffed grouse (1 per 2 persons)
salt
pepper
melted butter
paprika
flour or cornstarch

One of the easiest and yet most sumptuous ways to prepare ruffed grouse is by roasting. Each bird will serve two guests. Salt and pepper each whole bird and then place them in a shallow roasting pan to which ½ inch of hot water has been added so that they do not lose their moisture and juiciness. Next place the birds in a 350-degree pre-heated oven and brush them liberally with melted butter as they cook. The birds will probably have to bake for about 1 hour, but this depends upon their sizes, so continual checking of them is necessary. Just as the grouse are entering their final 15 minutes of roasting time, sprinkle them lightly with paprika. You can test for doneness by wiggling the legs and looking at the breasts. If the legs move easily, and the breasts are brown, remove the birds from the roasting pan and set them on a warming tray to stay hot.

Stir just a bit of flour or cornstarch into the liquid in the bottom of the pan until a rich gravy is formed. It is entirely a matter of per-

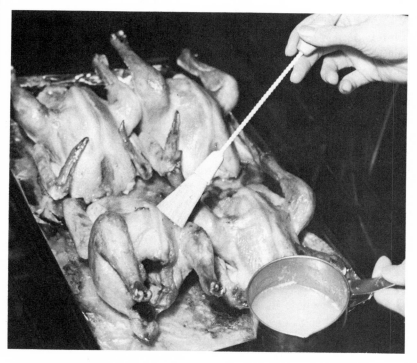

Many gamebirds can be roasted to perfection. It is wise to baste them frequently with melted butter.

sonal preference but we like to spoon this gravy over new potatoes, with a green or yellow vegetable side dish that is very mild and does not compete with the game.

Timberdoodle Treasure
8 whole woodcock
¼ cup cooking oil
2 cups water
1 cup sherry
4 teaspoons frozen concentrated orange juice
flour

With breast meat dark and leg meat light, the distinctive flavor of woodcock is usually one that can never be fully appreciated at first. It is something you must acquire a taste for, something you learn to love only after you have paid your dues for many years as a seasoned upland hunter. Yet Timberdoodle Treasure is one of those matchless efforts that upon first taste is immediately recognized for its high gourmet quality: it is not too foreign, not too familiar, obviously rich and special. Further, the recipe itself is quite simple.

Dust each whole woodcock with flour and then brown them on all sides in a covered pan containing ¼ cup of cooking oil. Now, reduce the heat, add 2 cups of water and 1 cup of sherry, cover the pan again and allow the birds to bubble slowly for 45 minutes.

When the birds are tender, remove them from the pan to some place where they will stay warm while you prepare a gravy liquor made by adding to the liquid in the cooking pan just a bit more water, just a bit more sherry, and 4 teaspoons frozen concentrated orange juice. Heat the liquor, while continually stirring, until it is steaming, and just before serving the birds ladle over the tops of them 1 full tablespoon of the sauce.

This dish is rich and full, so it is not wise to serve side dishes that may wage war with the main attraction. I suggest white rice and a mild yellow vegetable such as wax beans. Serves four.

Woodcock with Bacon
8 woodcock breasts
8 strips bacon

Only the very honest and humble deserve anything as good as Woodcock with Bacon, and as the old saw goes, "There aren't many of us left."

With this recipe, only the breasts are used and they can be broiled over charcoal or in your oven, or they can be roasted. Very simply, wrap each breast with a strip of bacon. Then submit the birds to the heat and remove them the minute the bacon just begins to turn brown so the woodcock breasts are never cooked beyond juicy medium-rare, as this is when they are at their tender and flavorful best. Recommended side dishes are baked potatoes and any green vegetable. Serves four.

Roast Pheasant with Wild Grape Sauce
    whole pheasant (1 per 3 persons)
    flour
    salt
    pepper
    paprika
    chicken or turkey stuffing

    4 cups wild grapes
    4 tablespoons butter, melted
    ¼ cup sherry
    3 whole cloves
    1 tablespoon lemon juice
    1 tablespoon grated lemon rind

Ringnecks are ideal for introducing gamebirds to first-timers who have never before savored such fare. The meat is tender and the flavor gentle yet distinctive. So if you are unsure as to whether your guests possess the educated taste for woodcock or the discernment to appreciate grouse, pheasant roasted in a manner similar to that of chicken or turkey is sure to draw accolades and applause. One cock ringneck will serve three very generously. But a cock that has seen the passing of several seasons may be tough, though just the opposite is usually true with partridge (an older cock grouse invariably being much more tender than a hen or yearling).

You can easily ascertain ahead of time whether a cock pheasant you have killed is an older bird and likely to require special attention. For one, the stiffness of the bill is a clue. If the bird can be lifted by the lower beak without its breaking, the ringneck is a mature adult. Also, if the spurs are hard and the claws blunt at their tips, the bird is a veteran and the meat may not be as tender as you would like unless you employ any of several remedies. However, a young pheasant's beak will be soft and its spurs pliable, yet its claws will be sharp.

As described in a previous chapter, permitting an older bird to hang and age for several days will improve its tenderness. Or, use a larding needle to impregnate the bird's flesh in random locations with melted butter or bacon fat, which serves to baste the meat internally during the cooking process. I also suggest using a commercial meat tenderizer, but the little-known trick to the effectiveness of meat tenderizer used on poultry is liberally sprinkling it not on the exterior of the bird but throughout the *inside* of the body cavity.

Roast Pheasant is one gamebird recipe in which I like to fill the body cavity with some type of stuffing. That which is commonly used with chicken or turkey is ideal.

In preparing the pheasant for the oven, make a mixture of sifted flour, salt, pepper and paprika, then rub this generously into the skin of the bird. Line a deep roasting pan with aluminum foil that comes up well over the sides. Set the pheasant in the bottom, then fashion a tent by bringing up the sides of the foil and pinching them on top to contain moisture during the roasting time (this also helps further to tenderize an older bird). Roast in a 350-degree oven until tender, then fold down the sides of the tent, raise the oven temperature to 375 degrees and permit the bird to brown for an additional half hour while basting frequently with the juices that have collected in the bottom of the pan.

In complementing your roast pheasant and dressing, a rather tart side dish is in order and I recommend several tablespoons per person of wild grape sauce. Wash 4 cups of wild grapes, cover with boiling water, simmer for 5 minutes, and drain. Now press the still-warm grapes through a sieve. In a sauce pan melt 4 tablespoons of butter, then add ¼ cup sherry, three whole cloves, and 1 tablespoon of lemon juice. Simmer these ingredients for 5 minutes, then remove the cloves and add the grape puree and 1 tablespoon of grated lemon rind. This excellent sauce can be served next to the pheasant on each person's plate or in small cocktail glasses.

The ringneck is not native to this country, having been imported from the Orient long ago. Yet it adapted well—even thrived as if it originally belonged here—and has provided countless upland gunners with innumerable hours of challenging excitement afield. Therefore, it seems only proper that Roast Pheasant be accompanied by a deep red, domestic burgundy.

Chukar in Sherry Sauce
breasts and legs of 4 chukar partridge
flour
cooking oil
medium-dry sherry

I have dined upon chukar partridge only one time and that meal consisted of four birds taken on a hunting preserve in northeastern Ohio. Though transplants have been attempted in many regions east of the Mississippi, only those gunners who are willing to visit the arid regions of the West are likely to see good sport with native birds.

A favorite gamebird recipe from Idaho hunter Billy Williams is Chukar in Sherry Sauce. It is beyond compare, but regularly dined upon only by those residing in Western states.

The chukars I killed were hung for two days, during which time I called my friend Billy Williams, a former Ohio resident now living in Idaho, for his favorite recipe...knowing full well he had become hopelessly addicted to hunting the species and likely had dined upon more chukar partridge during the last year than I expected to enjoy during an entire lifetime of upland gunning. Billy suggested Chukar in Sherry Sauce.

Lightly flour the breasts and legs of 4 birds, then brown in cooking oil. Pour several tablespoons of medium-dry sherry over the birds a little at a time as they continue to cook over very low heat with a lid covering the frypan. When the birds are tender (about 1 hour) remove them to a warming plate while making a gravy by adding water and just a touch more sherry to the pan. Then ladle the gravy over the breasts and legs and serve.

As might be expected with this dish, Billy prefers large Idaho baking potatoes, cooked in their jackets and then slit down the centers, with wedges of real butter inserted. A mild salad also goes well with this meal if you ensure that the ingredients are ice cold, cut into chunks (not diced!) and garnished sparingly with an unobtrusive dressing. Serves four.

Southern Doves
16 dove breasts
¼ cup butter or cooking oil
flour
salt
pepper

Most surely, I have spent more shells per bird killed when dove hunting than in gunning for any other species. And it is the uncertainty of the diving, careening flight antics of doves that see me coming back time and again to bust still more caps.

A South Carolina cotton farmer by the name of Ralph White introduced me to Southern Doves, explaining that the dish originated on poor farms where tenants were not given to spending money on fancy spices and "fixin's" and yet were known for their culinary triumphs.

First, shake the dove breasts in a brown paper bag containing a modest amount of flour. Then heat butter or cooking oil in the bottom of a skillet. Sear the birds quickly, turning them continually until they are well browned on all sides. Now, salt and pepper the breasts, turn the heat very low, add enough water to come halfway up on the birds, cover the pan and let the liquid bubble for 1½ hours. Lift out the birds when they are tender, thicken the gravy with flour, and serve with biscuits and any variety of "country vegetables" such as black-eyed peas or collard greens. Serves four.

Chestnut-stuffed Wild Turkey
1 whole wild turkey
½ pound sausage meat
½ cup chopped onion
1 cup chopped celery
½ cup water
1 teaspoon salt
½ teaspoon pepper
⅛ teaspoon crushed thyme
½ cup chopped parsley
1 cup chestnuts, cooked and chopped
8 cups chopped bread crumbs
bacon strips

Perhaps the most exciting of all upland game, and many times even classified as big game, is the wild turkey. Unfortunately, for the hunter anyway, the turkey is the most elusive of all gamebirds and therefore few gunners relish him on the dinner table with any degree of regularity.

Should you score in the near future, I would like to suggest Chestnut-stuffed Wild Turkey, and if the bird you have dropped is in the 12- to 14-pound range, you may invite eight close friends to share in the dining celebration with you.

First, pluck the bird and then hold it briefly over an open flame to singe off the remaining down. Now wipe the body cavity and the exterior of the bird with a hot, damp cloth. Lightly sprinkle the bird inside and out with salt and pepper and then set it aside briefly.

In a saucepan, cook the sausage meat until it's well done and then add the chopped onion, chopped celery, and water, and continue cooking on low heat until the vegetables are tender.

Now add the salt, pepper, crushed thyme, chopped parsley, chestnuts and chopped bread crumbs. Mix all of these ingredients thoroughly, using your hands if you like, and then spoon the stuffing into the neck and body cavities of the bird.

Close the neck and body openings with meat skewers or string, tie the legs up, tuck the wings under the body, and place the bird on a rack in a roasting pan. Cover the bird completely with bacon strips and roast in a 325-degree oven for ½ hour per pound.

To prevent the breast and upper portions of the legs from browning too quickly, you may have to cover the turkey with a sheet of foil for the first few hours of cooking. Basting every half hour with juices from the pan is advised. When the bird is tender, remove the loose drape of foil and turn the oven temperature up to 375 degrees to brown the breast.

In the case of long-bearded older birds – those weighing more than 14 pounds – one way to ensure tenderness is to roast the turkey in a brown paper bag. Use a regular large-size, heavy-duty grocery bag. Set the bird inside, close the end with a paper clip, then set the works on your roasting rack and cook in the usual way. The bag won't catch

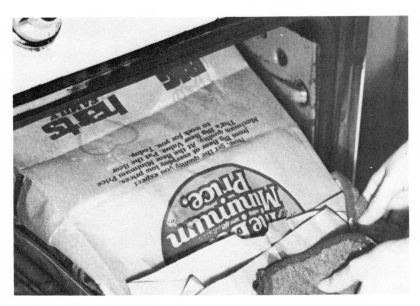

Of many ways to roast turkeys, one that ensures a tender bird is setting it in a brown paper bag before placing in your roasting pan. Don't worry, the bag won't catch fire, but it will lock in flavor and moisture.

fire in the oven or pose any other danger, but it will trap steam and make even the most ancient gobbler tender and mouth-watering.

Upon removing the turkey from the oven — no matter which cooking method you prefer — allow it to sit for ½ hour before carving. Excellent side dishes to accompany your prize, in addition to the chestnut dressing, are glazed sweet potatoes, chilled cranberry sauce and any green vegetable of your liking.

More Favorite Recipes

Just because the following recipes have been placed at the end of this chapter is no suggestion whatever that they take a back seat to the ones described earlier. They're recipes we use often, and I wouldn't put them here if there was any doubt regarding their wide acceptance among dedicated upland hunters.

Walt Rucker's Burgundy Doves
6 doves, split lengthwise to make 12 halves
2 cups red burgundy
½ teaspoon salt
¼ teaspoon black pepper

In a bowl, thoroughly mix the burgundy, salt and pepper. Then add the doves so they are completely covered with the liquid. Let the doves soak in the wine marinade for 1 hour, turning them every 15 minutes. Broil the doves over a bed of charcoal until the meat is just barely medium-rare (no more than 3 minutes per side). Serves four.

Doves with Mushrooms
8 dove breasts
1 cup butter
1 small onion, diced
1 cup mushrooms
1 cup red wine
¼ cup Worcestershire Sauce
salt
pepper

Rub just a bit of salt and pepper into the dove breasts, then brown them in a skillet with the butter. Remove the doves to a warm plate, then sauté the onions and mushrooms until they are tender. Stir in the wine and Worcestershire Sauce, then return the dove breasts to the skillet. Cover the pan with a lid and simmer on low heat for 1 hour. Serves four.

Crumb-coated Pheasant
2 pheasants, split in half lengthwise
½ cup sour cream
1 tablespoon garlic powder
2 cups crushed cheese crackers
½ teaspoon thyme
1 teaspoon salt
½ teaspoon black pepper

Thoroughly rub the pheasant halves with the sour cream. Then mix together the cheese crackers, thyme, salt, pepper and garlic powder. Roll the pheasant halves in the crumb mixture until they are thoroughly coated, then carefully lay them skin-side up in a glass baking dish or roasting pan lined with foil. Cover the dish with a lid, or the roasting pan with a sheet of foil, and set in an oven pre-heated to 350 degrees. Bake 45 minutes. At the end of the allotted baking time, remove the foil or baking dish lid and continue baking another 30 minutes or until the birds are tender. Serves six.

Savory Roast Pheasant
1 pheasant
1 bay leaf
1 lemon slice
1 can chicken broth
1 can mushrooms
1 large onion, sliced
4 bacon strips
1 clove garlic, crushed
¼ teaspoon celery seed
salt
pepper

Lightly rub a bit of salt and pepper inside the body cavity and on the outside of the bird. Place the lemon slice, celery seed, bay leaf and garlic inside the body cavity. Tie the legs together with cotton string, tuck the wings under the body, and place in a deep roasting pan. Cover the breast and legs of the pheasant with the bacon strips. Arrange the onion slices and mushrooms around the pheasant in the bottom of the pan, then carefully pour in the can of chicken broth. Roast in an oven pre-heated to 350 degrees for 30 minutes per pound, basting frequently with the juices from the pan. Serves three.

Quail with Orange Rice
8 quail, whole and plucked
1 cup butter or margarine, melted
1 cup apple jelly
½ cup cornstarch
1⅓ cups sauterne wine
½ cup orange juice
½ teaspoon salt
2 cups white seedless grapes
Orange Rice (described later)

In a skillet, brown the quail on all sides in the butter, then arrange the birds in the bottom of a roasting pan or large glass casserole dish. Melt the apple jelly over low heat and then set aside. Add the cornstarch to the drippings in the skillet, blending well. Stir in the melted apple jelly, sauterne, orange juice and salt. Cook on low heat, stirring continually until smooth and thickened. Pour the sauce over the quail and bake uncovered at 350 degrees for 1 hour. Then add the grapes and bake an additional 10 minutes or until the grapes are hot. Meanwhile, prepare the Orange Rice.

Orange Rice
2 cups diced celery with leaves
6 tablespoons chopped onion
½ cup butter or margarine, melted
2 cups uncooked Minute Rice
2½ cups boiling water
1½ cups orange juice
¼ cup grated orange rind
1 teaspoon salt

Sauté the onion and celery in the butter until they are clear. Stir the rice and salt into the boiling water, cover, and let sit 5 minutes. Add the orange juice, orange rind and sautéed vegetables. Cover and cook 5 minutes longer on low heat. Finally, remove the quail and place over the bed of rice on a large, heated serving platter. Serves four.

Quail with Flair
8 quail, whole and plucked
1½ cups butter or margarine
1 medium onion, minced
4 teaspoons flour
½ cup white wine
1½ cups chicken broth (canned)
salt
pepper

Rub the outside and inside of each bird with just a pinch of salt and pepper. Sauté the onion in a skillet containing the butter. Remove the onion to a plate and brown the birds in the same butter, then remove the quail and stir the flour into the butter. Next, stir in the wine and chicken broth. Place the quail and onions in a large glass casserole dish or foil-lined roasting pan. Pour the sauce over the tops of the birds. Then cover the dish with a lid, or the roasting pan with a sheet of foil, and bake at 300 degrees for 1½ hours or until tender. Serves four.

Deepfried Woodcock
8 woodcock, whole and plucked
1 cup flour
1 teaspoon salt
½ teaspoon pepper
cooking oil

Mix the salt and pepper together, then rub each bird inside and out with the seasoning. Place the flour in a brown paper bag and shake each bird individually until well coated. Fill a deep pot with cooking oil and heat it until it is very hot. Place two birds at a time in a wire basket (of the type used to make french fries) and then lower them into the hot oil for a total of 5 minutes. Remove the birds and place on absorbent paper toweling on a cookie sheet and set in your oven turned on low to keep warm while frying the remaining birds. Serves four.

Woodcock Breasts on Toast
8 woodcock breasts
1 teaspoon flour
½ teaspoon pepper
bacon strips
½ cup butter, melted
1 tablespoon parsley flakes
4 slices rye bread
1 teaspoon salt

Mix together the salt and pepper, then rub into the woodcock breasts. Wrap each breast with a strip of bacon, held in place with a toothpick. Place the breasts on a broiler pan 6 inches from the heat and broil 5 minutes on each side, basting frequently with the melted butter. Remove the toothpicks from the breasts and cut the bacon into small pieces. Toast the rye bread, sprinkle the bacon bits on top, then lay two woodcock breasts on top of each slice, sprinkle lightly with parsley and serve. Serves four.

Al Wolter's Upland Bird Casserole
1 box Uncle Ben's Long Grain & Wild Rice
  (makes 4 cups)
2 cups woodcock and grouse meat
1 can condensed cream of mushroom soup
¼ cup chopped celery
½ teaspoon salt
¼ teaspoon black pepper

This recipe is ideal when a hunter has leftover legs and other body parts from grouse and woodcock, although you can cut up entire birds as the combination of white grouse breast meat and dark woodcock meat join to make an unparalleled marriage of dining excellence. Cut the meat into small pieces. Cook the wild rice per instructions on the package. When the rice is done, thoroughly mix in the meat and ingredients and stir until completely blended. Then spoon into a buttered casserole dish, cover with a lid, and bake in an oven preheated to 350 degrees for 30 minutes. Serves four.

11

Field Care and Butchering of Small Game

There are those who use predator calls to lure foxes, bobcats and coyotes to the gun. In these cases the animals are hunted mainly for their pelts and are looked upon as-not having palatable meat.

Then there are groundhogs, woodchucks, opossums and raccoons that, when young and prepared with certain specialized recipes, do indeed provide excellent eating.

But take a poll of the country's sportsmen, asking how they began their hunting careers, and it's predictable that rabbits will be mentioned more often than not. The actual species may have been any of the 30 known cottontail strains, the several jackrabbit subspecies, or even one of the hares such as the snowshoe variety, but any kid toting a .22 rifle or .410 shotgun afield for the very first time undoubtedly has high hopes of encountering some type of rabbit or another.

I'd also be willing to bet that of the sportsmen who didn't as a youngster fire their first hunting shot at a rabbit, there would be virtually unanimous agreement that the quarry of their seeking was either gray or fox squirrels.

It's understandable why rabbits and squirrels are the first game animals to capture a budding hunter's interest. The two inhabit every state, which means they enjoy a national popularity among young hunters. Also, in any given region, rabbits and squirrels generally are so prolific that a boy or girl on their first outing with Dad (or some other relative) stands an excellent chance of at least seeing game, if not actually getting a shot at it, every time out. This generates an enthusiasm for hunting that can be acquired in no other way, and causes young outdoorsmen to want to return to favorite woodlots and briar patches time and time again. Another advantage of either rabbits or squirrels as the first species hunted is that while they can be elusive and cagey at times, they are not tremendously difficult to bag. With a bit of proper instruction from an adult, and patience, success is likely to come rather quickly, which also is necessary if a continued interest in hunting is to be nurtured. Finally, of the many reasons hunters pursue game, bringing home food for the table is an intrinsic part of the sport. And when it comes to good eating, rabbits and squirrels are near the very top of the list.

Yet it should be made clear that rabbit and squirrel hunting aren't something that appeal only to young hunters. I know grandfathers with more than 50 years of hunting behind them who still look upon squirrel hunts with as much excitement as the day they bagged their first bushytail at age nine. There is one doddering old gentleman in our neck of the woods who turns his beagles loose and then must use a cane to follow. While it is sometimes difficult to define the magic attraction of rabbit and squirrel hunting, the interest, once acquired, is seldom outgrown. Maybe one reason is because in these days of expensive, time-consuming hunts for more glamorous species such as elk, hunting rabbits and squirrels remains as uncomplicated as it ever was. Almost any gun will do, and you can go on the spur of the moment whenever a particularly sun-drenched afternoon holds promise. Even if you live in a big city, you're certain to be within an hour's drive of good rabbit and squirrel hunting. If you live in a small town, reduce that time to 15 minutes, and if you live in the country the critters are probably within 100 yards of your back door.

However, none of this is meant to diminish the importance of proper field care of the quarry. The game may be small but it still deserves the utmost consideration if the final taste test is to be rewarding. Even the most renowned chef is always limited by the quality and condition of the meat handed him.

Cool the Meat Quickly

A traditional part of Thanksgiving Day on our southern Ohio farm is a low-key rabbit hunt. By low-key, I mean that we don't really care if we kill game. The important thing is simply to be outdoors with friends or relatives on a special day on which we're giving thanks for many things – including the privilege to hunt – and while doing so listening to the music of hounds as they bellow out a chorus that is as old as time. If someone does indeed kill a rabbit, it's merely an unexpected bonus in an already richly fulfilled day.

We seldom have much concern for field care of rabbits taken under such circumstances, the reason being that the weather usually is chilly, if not downright frigid and laced with driving sleet and snow. Besides, we know we'll be back at my farmhouse sipping hot buttered rum within the hour. So all that's really necessary is to field-strip the rabbit of its insides, wipe out the body cavity with dry grass and tuck it into a game bag for the brief remainder of the hunt and the hike home.

The same can be said of squirrel hunting at dawn when sparkles of frost litter the ground like broken crystal, or any other time when nature provides instant refrigeration for one's game.

Yet there are just as many other situations in which unseasonably warm temperatures prevail. In Ohio and many other midwestern states, for example, the squirrel season begins around September 15th and although we have a few times seen the opener greeted with snow, it is far more customary for the midday mercury to push the 80 degree mark. There are states where, due to their southerly latitudes, it may be downright scorching hot almost any time one chooses to pursue small game. I remember one time I was chasing jackrabbits across an Arizona saguaro flat in such blistering temperatures that I had to wear three pairs of socks to prevent my boot soles from burning my feet. I later learned it was 107 degrees that day!

In these latter situations it is crucial that any game killed be given immediate attention. In fact, a good way to tackle this whole business of field care of small-game meat is to keep in mind *The Rule of 15* which I coined a number of years ago. It means that with each 15-degree increase in the air temperature, game meat must be accordingly given a different type of treatment.

– If the air temperature is *15°* or less, some type of measure must be taken to prevent the meat from freezing.

– If the air temperature is *15°* to *30°*, simple gutting of the animal is sufficient until such time as later dressing operations can be attended to.

– If the air temperature is *30°* to *45°*, gut the animal and plan to remove the hide within one hour.

– If the air temperature is *45°* to *60°*, gut the animal and remove the hide immediately.

– If the air temperature is *60°* or *more*, gut the animal, remove the hide, and immediately seek additional cooling measures such as a cooler filled with crushed ice.

Follow this simple guideline and no matter where you hunt or which small-game species draws your interest, your quarry is ensured of remaining fresh and flavorful.

Field-Dressing Squirrels and Rabbits

Hunters often take entirely different approaches in field-dressing rabbits and squirrels. I am not exactly sure why this is so – maybe it's because squirrel hunters usually are sitting somewhere, while rabbit hunters are usually on the move.

In the case of bushytails, all that's really necessary is to lay the carcass across your lap, belly up, and with the thumb and forefinger grab the abdominal skin and lift. Then with the tip of your knife, blade edge facing up so as to not cut too deeply, slit open the belly from the anus to the beginning of the rib cage. It's now an easy task to insert two fingers far up into the chest cavity, grab the heart and lungs and begin stripping them out, following with the intestines and lower organs, which may have to be severed free in the pelvic region. Next grab a small handful of dry grass and wipe the body cavity of any remaining blood or fluids.

After this, I usually like to lay the squirrel on the ground next to me, on its back, with a small stick spreading the body cavity walls to speed cooling.

This same, simple procedure can be used on rabbits as well, or any small game for that matter. But an even easier method for bunnies is to cut a 1½-inch slit in the lower abdomen region. Then grab the rabbit with both hands high on the rib cage, squeeze slightly, and with a snap of your wrist swing the rabbit in exactly the same manner as if you were swinging a baseball bat. The entrails will literally shoot right out of the abdominal cut as though you had smacked a line drive to center field. Again, use a few pinches of dry grass or moss to wipe out the body cavity.

Following *The Rule of 15*, nothing else in the way of field dress-

The first step in field-dressing cottontails is to enlarge the vent area slightly with your knife. Then squeeze the rib cage firmly and swing the rabbit like a baseball bat. The entrails will go flying like a line drive to center field.

ing may be required if the temperature is cool or cold. If it's warm, plan to remove the hide within an hour, following the instructions we'll give in a moment. If it's hot, remove the hide immediately; the carcass can be kept clean in your game bag by placing it in a plastic bag that has numerous inch-long slits in it to facilitate the circulation of air and prevent the build-up of warm, moist condensation. When hunting in such conditions there should be a cooler waiting back at your car or camp, filled with crushed ice. I like to plan my rabbit and squirrel hunts so that I make looping passes that leave camp (or home, or car) but after an hour or so begin to swing back in the same direction from which I've just come. This allows me now and then to be close enough to stop conveniently at my car or camp for a moment to deposit in my cooler any game that may have been taken.

Another option in hot weather, if you may be an hour or more away from your cooler, is to skip the step of cutting small slices in the plastic bag holding the game and instead secure the neck, then place the bag in a spring-fed brook or stream. Hold the bag down with a rock, or tie it to a shoreline root or stump, and the cool rushing water will keep the meat in good condition all day or until such time as you can return to your car.

We should mention that squirrels and rabbits sometimes carry parasites, and the hunter should know what to look for and how to differentiate those which are harmless from those which may be dangerous.

In the case of squirrels, an occasional animal may evidence warbles, which appear as one or more unsightly lumps, usually around the shoulders and legs. Many hunters discard these squirrels, thinking the animal is diseased and dangerous, but this is not true at all. The swollen-looking lumps are caused by the warble fly, which lays its eggs on tree bark, and when the eggs hatch the larvae transfer to the first passing squirrel. The larva burrows under the skin where it grows into a large grub, hence the lump. Although rather grotesque looking, such lumps do not affect the meat in any way, and come right off when the squirrel later is skinned and butchered. It's also worth noting that warble fly activity is characteristic of warm weather, and after the first hard frost squirrels found to be affected by the parasite are quite rare.

Squirrels also may be infected by mange or scabies, caused by the scabies mite. This often is fatal to them because the squirrels scratch themselves until their bodies are bloody and hairless, which weakens them and makes them more susceptible to predation and the elements. I suggest that mange-infected squirrels not be added to the game bag, as the infections may have penetrated deep into their musculature. Just leave them lay (birds and other scavengers will appreciate the free meal) or bury them.

With rabbits, tularemia often causes great concern, but it need not. Occasionally a rabbit with tularemia is discovered, but biologists claim less than 1 in 10,000 rabbits is so afflicted. A rabbit that has tularemia will reveal very lethargic behavior so that it seems sluggish and not wanting to move or run. Also, when dressing a tularemic rabbit the hunter will note hundreds of tiny white spots on an enlarged and swollen liver. If these are ever noted, bury the animal at once, handling it minimally, then wash your hands thoroughly because tularemia is contagious and may be passed from animals to humans.

The white spots we're talking about here should not be mistaken for other white spots more commonly seen that are far fewer in number: half a dozen, not hundreds. They are about the size of an eraser on the end of a pencil, and when they appear on a normal-size liver, in a rabbit that behaves normally, they evidence what's called the "dog tapeworm." Further clues of the tapeworm's presence may be little white objects about the size of a grain of rice, which are encased in envelopes of clear jelly. They may be scattered throughout the body cavity but are most commonly seen in the pelvic region.

These little white cysts are not harmful to humans, and the great majority come away during the course of normal field dressing and most of the rest during skinning and butchering. However, there is one matter of great importance. Nature's way of transferring these tapeworms to new victims is for the victim to devour the dormant cyst while eating some type of food. Rabbits, then, are only intermediate hosts between members of the canine clan in the life cycle of the dog tapeworm, so at all costs do not allow your hunting dog to eat discarded entrails. Curiously this is something many small-game hunters (bird hunters, too) allow, which should be discouraged.

Two other afflictions of rabbits are the botfly larva, a 1½-inch creature that burrows under the skin and causes a lump, usually in the neck or shoulder region, and Shope's fibroma, a soft, pink wart that sometimes appears on the face or feet. Both are unsightly but harmless to humans and removed with cleaning.

In describing these afflictions of rabbits and squirrels, it is not my intention to alarm hunters. On the contrary, the above diseases and infestations are quite uncommon (in my 30 years of small-game hunting I've twice encountered squirrels with warbles, but never experienced any of the other parasites mentioned, nor any of the diseases). But since there is indeed the slight possibility that a hunter may encounter some abnormality in the small game he kills, he should know how to identify those which are harmful and those which are not.

Skinning Small Game

Of all the small-game species, rabbits are the easiest and fastest to skin, simply because the critters' hides are so thin and soft. As a matter of fact, it's sometimes difficult to remove a rabbit's skin in one piece because it tears so easily. Just the opposite is true with squirrels as their far more leathery skin can require implemention of the old Armstrong method of hide removal.

In any event, the skin of any small-game animal becomes increasingly more difficult to remove as time passes and it is allowed to stiffen. And since little advantage is gained by aging small-game meat, other than the small degree of additional tenderness that may be attributed to sitting in a refrigerator for a day or two before cooking, sound advice is to remove the skin at the first convenient opportunity.

With small-game animals such as raccoons and opossums you'll probably want to hang the animal by the head or hind legs and carefully take off the skin as you would from any furbearer, because the pelts from such creatures are worth a handy bit of cash.

There is no value in rabbit or squirrel skins, although you can sell accumulated squirrel tails to fishing lure manufacturers (contact Sheldon's, P.O. Box 508, Antigo, Wisconsin 54409) and a fly-tying friend may occasionally like to have a quantity of rabbit fur.

For removing the skin from a rabbit, here is the easiest method I've ever come across:

First, with your thumb and forefinger grab a fold of skin where it is loose along the shoulders or back region, lift, and make a 2-inch slit perpendicular to the backbone. Trying to "saw" through rabbit fur is a futile endeavor, so just insert the tip of your knife blade to make

1. To remove a rabbit's skin, make a shallow cut across the back, being careful not to cut too deeply into the meat.

2. Then insert two fingers of each hand into the cut you've made and pull your hands in opposite directions. The soft skin will quickly peel away.

3. The next step is to remove the head by cutting straight down through the neck.

4. Then use shears to cut off all four lower legs.

a small hole, then lengthen it by slicing, being careful not to damage the tenderloin meat directly underneath.

Second, insert two or three fingers from each hand into the slit and then begin pulling your hands apart in opposite directions. Steady pulling in this manner will see the hide peel right off the carcass as easily as if you were pulling off your hunting socks. If the skin happens to rip or tear someplace, no problem. Just grab a loose flap of the skin here or there and pull it away with your fingers.

Third, continue pulling in opposite directions and the skin will pull up and over the head and front shoulders at one end, and down the hind legs at the other.

Fourth, just behind the head cut through the neck meat until you reach the neck bone, then sever the bone with your knife or use a pair of shears, or twist the head to break the bone.

Fifth, the head should now still be attached to a flap of skin in the lower neck region, and continued pulling will see the hide peel cleanly down the front legs. Somewhere below the knees, just above the paws, cut the leg bones with shears.

Sixth, cut a V-notch in the region of the anus to remove that organ as well as the tail. A bit of further pulling on the skin down the hind legs and you can then sever the leg bones the same way as you did those at the front of the carcass.

You should now have a completely skinned rabbit carcass, free of its insides, legs, head and tail. Further butchering operations are the same as with squirrels or other small game, so let's look first at skinning squirrels, which differs slightly.

As we noted earlier, a squirrel's hide is firmly attached. If the squirrel is still warm after just being killed, or is a young animal, you can skin it in exactly the same way as just described for rabbits, although considerably more pulling strength will have to be employed.

However, if it has been an hour or so since the squirrel was killed, or if it is an older animal, a different strategy is much better.

First, lay the squirrel on its belly. Lift up the tail and cut through the tail bone with your knife, being careful to cut only the skin just below the tail and not that on top of the tail along the back.

Second, this cut, which has been made just beneath the tail and perpendicular to the backbone, should now be extended down the squirrel's flanks on each side, following the slight depression that is just in front of the hind legs, all the way to the lengthwise abdominal cut made when field-dressing the animal.

Third, firmly grab a hind leg in each hand, step heavily on the tail to hold it securely against the ground, and slowly pull upward. What you're doing here is using two opposing forces, and the skin will slowly peel down and away for the length of the body, eventually going over the front shoulders and legs and then down the neck.

Fourth, still holding the tail down with your foot for leverage, work your fingers under the skin of each hind leg and begin pulling back and the skin will peel all the way down the hind legs.

Fifth, use a knife, or shears, to cut away each leg bone just above the paws, and then cut through the neck bone. What you should have after this is a completely skinned carcass in one hand, and the entire hide, head and feet, still attached to each other, lying on the ground.

Several times I've mentioned the use of shears, and now it might be wise to say a few more words on the subject.

You can purchase from stores that specialize in kitchen equipment a wide variety of such shears, that look not unlike heavy-duty scissors but have shorter, thicker, scimitar-shaped blades. They come in handy for numerous kitchen chores, but the better brands can be quite expensive. If you've got the dough to spend, fine, but if not, a good substitute is a pair of small tin snips sold in any hardware store.

The main advantage of using such shears for cleaning and dressing small game (as well as upland gamebirds and waterfowl) is that they are perfect for neatly snipping off feet and wings, cutting through leg bones, cutting ribs, severing backbones and neck bones, and even jointing cuts of meat into serving size portions. You see, when using a knife for many of these chores, considerable pressure often must be exerted and this increases the likelihood of the blade slipping and perhaps cutting your own carcass as well. Also, a knife doesn't always sever bones and joints cleanly but often shatters or crushes them and leaves jagged edges exposed.

Tin snips, or shears, make clean cuts. In fact, I find they even come in handy when I'm in the final stages of butchering big-game

1. Skinning is more difficult with squirrels than rabbits because their hide is far more securely attached. Begin by making a shallow cut underneath the tail.

2. Extend this cut down both flanks, through the notch where the hind legs meet the abdomen, and then connect the cut to the abdominal slice made when field-dressing the animal.

3. Now, put a foot securely on the tail and lift up on the carcass. This creates two opposing forces to pull the skin from the animal.

4. After the skin has been pulled over the front shoulders and legs and down the hind legs, use shears to cut the leg bones.

4.

5. A completely skinned, undamaged squirrel carcass should look like this.

5.

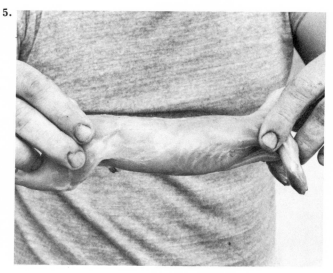

animals and have to periodically trim sinew, ligaments and so on. One hunter I know, who pursues gamebirds and small game with such passion that I'm continually amazed, even has made a small leather sheath for his tin snips, so he always has them with him on his belt right beside his knife.

The best part of using shears or tin snips is that you don't have to sharpen them constantly as you do a knife. However, after each use I do recommend rinsing them with scalding hot water so they don't serve as a breeding ground for bacteria.

Butchering Small Game

With a completely skinned and rough-dressed squirrel or rabbit carcass, the hunter will now want to section the meat into cooking-size pieces or those suitable for freezing.

Many hunters like merely to quarter their meat, or divide it into four roughly equal pieces.

First, lay the rabbit or squirrel on its back and, using shears, cut lengthwise through the rib cage from the breastbone to the neck.

Second, spread the chest walls apart with your hands and then place the tip of your knife blade right in the center of the backbone (inside the body cavity) and push down. The backbone should begin to split apart right down the middle, and the cut can be lengthened in both directions through additional knife cutting or the use of shears.

Third, with the animal halved lengthwise, each half is then cut in half, to produce quarters. That is, you'll have four pieces of meat (actually five, if you cut the neck meat free, which is optional): the left rear leg and part of the rear-backbone meat, the right rear leg and part of the rear-backbone meat, the left front leg and shoulder and part of the front-backbone meat, and the right front leg and shoulder and part of the front-backbone meat.

The one drawback to this method is that often the backbone has a somewhat jagged appearance. Also, the resulting quarters, especially in the case of rabbits, are just a bit too large to handle when engaging in various cooking operations, not to mention later eating activities (a quarter from a snowshoe hare or jackrabbit can be an enormous piece of meat).

I usually prefer an entirely different method of cutting up rabbits and squirrels that takes a bit longer but results in nicer looking cuts of meat that are easy to handle.

First, lay the rabbit or squirrel on its side with its backbone facing toward you. With the tip of your knife blade remove each hind leg. This is easily accomplished by cutting around each leg all the way down to the ball-and-socket joint, then going right between the two to cut the ligament there. When doing this cutting, keep your knife blade as close as possible to the backbone, so that no meat is wasted.

Second, remove the two front legs and shoulders by laying the knife blade flat and running it just beneath the scapula or shoulder bone. The anatomy here is just like that of a deer and the entire leg and shoulder should come away easily within a few seconds.

Third, cut off the neck-meat section by cutting straight down through it, perpendicular to the backbone just in front of the front shoulder.

To butcher either rabbits or squirrels, begin by removing the hind legs, keeping the knife blade close to the backbone and merely following the leg's contour. The front legs are easily removed by guiding the blade beneath the scapulae. Then, depending upon the size of the animal, you may want to cut the remaining back portion in half.

Fourth, with a pair of shears, cut off the pelvis, just in front of where it previously joined the rear legs.

Fifth, attend to the remaining, long piece of backbone that previously ran from the front shoulders to just before the pelvis. If this is rather small, as in the case of young squirrels, leave it as one piece. If it is large, as on a cottontail, cut it in half to make two equal pieces (front and back). If it's extremely large, as on a jackrabbit or hare, cut it into three equal pieces.

Sixth, using shears, trim away a bit of the lower rib cage and any remaining flaps of abdominal wall skin.

Whichever method you prefer, the meat sections should now be rinsed clean with cold water. If any hairs from the hide happen to be still adhering to the meat, they can easily be removed by blotting with a paper towel.

Of course, if there are any seriously damaged pieces of meat, trim them away with your knife, and remove any shot pellets you see lodged just beneath the surface of the meat.

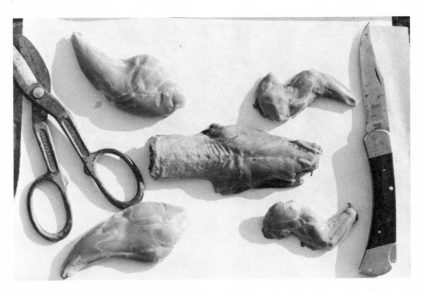

With either a rabbit or squirrel, your butchered pieces should look like this. Here, the backbone, taken from a squirrel and therefore somewhat small, has been left in one piece. With cottontails, you may desire to halve this section; with big jackrabbits or snowshoe hares you may even decide to quarter it.

Any other places where there is minor discoloration due to blood pockets should next be attended to. The easiest way is by just barely pricking the skin with the tip of your knife and rinsing the area with cold water. For pieces of meat that reveal deeper bloodshot areas that are salvageable, again prick the meat but then soak the meat overnight in a bowl of salt water.

At this time, you can pick a favorite recipe and get on with the business of cooking. Or, the meat will remain in good condition in your refrigerator for up to three days by placing it on a plate and covering with a handful of paper toweling that has been soaked with water and then wrung out.

No matter how much I like freshly killed rabbit and squirrel, it seems this additional bit of aging time in the refrigerator improves both the flavor and tenderness. Tenderness also can be improved by certain cooking methods (described in the next chapter) as well as freezing for two or three months.

12

Big Feasts with Little Critters

There is something enchanting about cooking small game. Maybe it has to do with that large part of our hunting heritage that is so deeply rooted in the remote hill-country of the Appalachians, Ozarks and Great Smoky Mountains, where for generations squirrel, rabbit, 'possum and 'coon suppers have not merely been the celebrations of sportsmen but a basic way of life. Indeed, a vast number of the most famous small-game recipes in existence today were devised by folks just trying to make do, who still cook over wood stoves and never have even heard of a Cuisinart Food Processor or a microwave oven.

However, rural Americans aren't the only ones who have long appreciated the sumptuous dinners that result when the main ingredient is small game. Hasenpfeffer is just one example of a recipe that long ago filtered its way from the Old World to this side of the ocean and to this day remains one of the most delicious ways of preparing rabbit. Incidentally, even in our Space Age world, a majority of Europeans still favor rabbit meat over domestic beef.

Yet small game is like the proverbial little girl in the old quip that goes, "When she is good she is very, very good and when she is bad she is horrid." What I mean is, among a majority of sportsmen and their families, there probably arise fewer complaints about strong or gamey flavors from small game than any other game meat. But the matter of tenderness may be an altogether different story, as anyone can attest who has tried to gnaw upon an old rogue of a squirrel that has sizzled to shoe-leather hardness in a frying pan.

Taming this toughness, evident to some degree in just about all but the very youngest of small-game animals, is no more complicated than using specialized cooking methods in accordance with the age of the animal in question.

214

Marinades and Parboiling

Soaking the game in a marinade for 24 hours will do a splendid job of tenderizing older animals, but keep in mind the particular marinade used will impart the meat with a twinge of its own unique flavor. Since I and most others relish the natural flavor of most small-game species, and don't want anything detracting from that flavor, I usually employ a marinade only as a last resort, when I'm confident the animal I've bagged is a grizzled old codger that absolutely will have to be marinated to be chewable.

Following are the two best marinade recipes I've come across in recent years.

Preparing a marinade is an excellent way to tenderize small-game meat that otherwise might be tough. Generally, the meat soaks in the marinade overnight in your refrigerator.

Simple Marinade
1 quart cold water
2½ tablespoons salt
3 tablespoons vinegar
¼ teaspoon pepper

Mix the ingredients thoroughly. Place quartered or sectioned meat pieces in a deep glass bowl, pour the marinade over the top, cover with a lid and set in your refrigerator for 24 hours.

Fancy Wine Marinade
2 cups dry red wine
¼ cup vinegar
1 small onion, chopped
1 medium carrot, diced
¼ teaspoon pepper
1 bay leaf, broken
2 stalks celery, chopped
½ cup cooking oil
1 tablespoon parsley flakes

Mix all the ingredients thoroughly, pour over meat in a glass bowl, cover with a lid, and set in your refrigerator for 24 hours.

It's worth mentioning two types of marinades that offer a tenderizing effect without imparting any flavors of their own. One is the popular Baking Soda Marinade, which entails the mixing of 1 quart of cold water, ½ cup baking soda, and 1 teaspoon salt. Simply blend the ingredients until the soda and salt are dissolved in the water, then pour over the meat in the usual way.

The second is the Buttermilk Marinade which, again, tenderizes meat but leaves behind no residual flavors of its own. Place small-game pieces in a glass bowl, cover with buttermilk, place a lid on the bowl, then set in your refrigerator overnight.

With regard to any of these marinades, it should be emphasized that only deep glass bowls with rather tight-fitting lids are suitable. Plastic or metal bowls may be damaged by a strong marinating solution, and there is the great possibility that the deterioration of the bowl's material may give the meat an unpleasant flavor. Also, during the course of marinating small game, be sure to turn the meat occasionally (every 6 or 8 hours is ideal). When the small-game meat is finished marinating for the prescribed length of time, remove it from the solution, pat the meat dry with paper toweling to absorb any of the liquid, then proceed with any recipe of your choosing.

Parboiling is another method of tenderizing meat for those who either don't care for marinades or don't have the time to wait for a 24-hour soaking period. Parboiling is simply adding pieces of meat to salted, boiling water, covering with a lid, bringing to a boil a second time, reducing the heat slightly, then cooking gently for 20 or 30 minutes before removing the meat, patting it dry, and proceeding with some other recipe.

Regarding the numerous recipes that follow in the next section, it is generally wise to use a *dry heat* cooking method with those small-game animals that are young and therefore tender. By dry heat, we mean panfrying, roasting or broiling. With the panfrying method there will likely be some type of batter, dip or coating to lock in flavor and juices, but when roasting or broiling small-game meat, occasionally basting the meat will ensure tenderness. I often like to use melted, heated bacon fat or beef suet, but for a pure, unadulterated wild-game flavor nothing beats the juices that have collected in the bottom of the pan.

Yet with older animals that are likely to be somewhat tough, even after undergoing a marinating period, a *moist heat* cooking method is far more desirable. Moist heat tenderizes the meat in its own juices, or in other liquids which are part of the particular recipe, as in braising, stewing and slow simmering in soups and casseroles.

Favorite Rabbit Recipes

Rabbit meat is delicious, and so it is not surprising that non-hunters in this country and abroad began domestically raising various species long ago in order to dine upon rabbit regularly. In fact, visit any small-town grocery store in the Midwest or South and you'll find dressed rabbits in the meat counter right beside the hamburger and chicken. Of course, sportsmen are lucky in that they can do their "shopping" for rabbit in the nearest grown-over field or briar patch. Of the thousands (yes, thousands!) of rabbit recipes that have evolved over the last 200 years, following are the ones I consider the most delicious.

Hasenpfeffer

2 rabbits, cut into pieces
¼ cup sour cream
2 tablespoons flour
½ cup water
1 small bay leaf
3 whole cloves
½ teaspoon paprika
½ teaspoon Accent monosodium glutamate
1 medium green pepper, chopped
1 medium onion, chopped
4 teaspoons tomato sauce
1½ teaspoons salt
¼ teaspoon black pepper
1 cup rabbit broth (see below)

Brown the meat on all sides in a skillet containing bacon fat. When the meat is brown, transfer it to a deep pot and turn the heat on low. Now add the onion, green pepper, salt, black pepper, tomato sauce, paprika, cloves, bay leaf, Accent and rabbit broth. The rabbit broth is made by placing trimmings of rabbit meat in a pot — use the belly section, ribs, even cut-up front leg if you wish — adding just enough water to cover (about 1½ cups) and simmering slowly for 30 minutes.

With all of the above ingredients added to the pot, cover with a lid and let the works bubble slowly for 1½ hours. Turn the meat every so often and at the same time check the liquid to make sure there still is enough; if not, add just a bit more rabbit broth or hot water.

The meat is done when it pierces easily when tested with a fork. When the meat is finished, transfer it to a large plate and set it in your oven to keep warm. With a slotted spoon remove the bay leaf and the cloves from the liquid in the pot. Then stir into the liquid a paste made by blending the 2 tablespoons of flour with ½ cup water. Continue stirring on low heat until a thick gravy has formed, then add the sour cream and continue stirring for several more minutes.

For an authentic hasenpfeffer dinner, the cooked rabbit meat should be served with dumplings. To make the dumplings, first set a large pot of lightly salted water on the stove and turn the heat high so it will come to a rolling boil. Meanwhile, break three eggs into a mixing bowl, add ¼ cup cold water and stir until they are well mixed. Then stir in just enough flour to make a silky, medium-thin dough. As soon as the water begins boiling, hold the bowl of dough over the pot and with a spoon cut off dumpling-size pieces of dough. As the individual pieces of dough hit the hot water they will sink momentarily, then float to the surface and swell up to two or three times their original size. When you have as many dumplings in the pot as your family can eat, cover the pot with a lid and let them steam just a short while on low heat. They should be done in about 7 minutes, but after 5 minutes I like to test one just to make sure they do not cook beyond the tender stage. Finally, place the rabbit on a platter, surround the meat with the dumplings, then ladle the gravy over both. Serves four.

Baked Rabbit
2 rabbits, cut into pieces
1 stick margarine
Kellogg's Cornflake Crumbs

If the rabbit is old and suspected to be tough, first marinate or parboil the meat. Then melt the stick of margarine in a shallow bowl or pan. Thoroughly rub each piece of rabbit in the melted margarine, then roll in the cornflake crumbs until well coated all over. Arrange the rabbit pieces on a well-greased cookie sheet or in a shallow pan and bake in an oven pre-heated to 350 degrees for 1 hour. Serves four.

Fried Rabbit
2 rabbits, cut into pieces
cold water
¼ cup vinegar
2 teaspoons salt
flour
cooking oil

Place the rabbit pieces in a deep pot, add the vinegar, then add cold water until the rabbit is just barely covered. Bring to a boil and cook 5 minutes. Then, *throw this water away*. Add the salt to the pot and more fresh, cold water until the rabbit pieces are covered, bring

After marinating, small game can be prepared in countless ways. One of the author's recommendations is frying until crispy brown.

to a boil, reduce the heat just a bit, and continue to cook until the rabbit pieces are almost tender. Then remove the pieces of rabbit, dredge thoroughly with flour (or corn meal, or cracker crumbs) and fry in a skillet in hot oil as you would chicken.

Shenandoah Valley Rabbit Casserole
  2 rabbits, cut into pieces
  bacon strips
  ½ teaspoon thyme
  3 large bay leaves, crumbled
  ½ teaspoon salt
  ¼ teaspoon black pepper
  1 cup water
  1 cup seasoned breadcrumbs

The Marlin Firearms Company in New Haven, Connecticut, not only makes a wide variety of rifles and shotguns but of late has been describing many famous recipes in its catalog. Shenandoah Valley Rabbit Casserole is one of the most delicious I've ever tried (but also treat your taste buds to the next recipe as well). Begin by soaking the rabbit pieces in salt water. Use a ratio of 1 teaspoon of salt per quart of cold water; soak young rabbits for 2 hours, older ones for 12 hours. After the prescribed soaking period, wrap the pieces of meat in a damp cloth and place in your refrigerator overnight. The next day, thoroughly smear the inside of a deep glass casserole dish with butter, then add a layer of rabbit pieces. Mix together the thyme, crumbled bay leaves, salt, and pepper and lightly sprinkle the meat. Now cover the meat with about 5 strips of bacon. Then add another layer of rabbit meat, sprinkle with the spice mixture again, add more bacon and so on until all of the rabbit pieces and seasonings are used up. Pour the cup of water over the top, cover the dish, and bake in an oven preheated to 350 degrees until the meat is tender (1 to 2 hours, depending upon the age of the rabbits). When the meat pierces easily with a fork, remove the lid, sprinkle the bread crumbs over the top, then bake an additional 30 minutes. Serves four.

Sour Cream Rabbit with Herbs
2 rabbits, cut into pieces
salt
pepper
flour
3 tablespoons butter
3 tablespoons olive oil
4 medium onions, sliced
2 cups beef bouillon
2 teaspoons tomato paste
½ cup sour cream
1 tablespoon chopped parsley
2 teaspoons chopped dill

Soak the rabbit pieces in salt water for 2 hours. Remove, pat dry with toweling, rub a bit of salt and pepper into each piece, then dust with flour. Add the butter and olive oil to a skillet and on medium heat brown the rabbit pieces on all sides. Transfer the rabbit pieces to a plate and place in your oven where they will stay hot. Then reduce the heat under the skillet and sauté the onion slices until they are clear. Add the beef bouillon and simmer 5 minutes on medium-high heat. Reduce the heat and stir in the tomato paste. Place the rabbit pieces back in the pan with the above ingredients, cover, and simmer slowly for 1 hour. When the meat is tender, place on a serving platter. Then in the pan juices, stir in 1 tablespoon flour, 2 tablespoons water and the sour cream. Stir until thoroughly hot. Ladle this sauce over the rabbit pieces and then sprinkle with the parsley and dill before serving. Serves four.

Country Rabbit with Mushrooms

2 rabbits, cut into pieces
2 cans condensed cream of mushroom soup
½ teaspoon salt
¼ teaspoon pepper
flour
1 medium onion, chopped
1 cup mushrooms

Dredge the rabbit pieces in flour, then brown in a frypan containing melted bacon fat, butter or cooking oil. Lay the rabbit pieces in the bottom of a buttered glass casserole baking dish, sprinkle with the salt and pepper, add the mushroom soup (undiluted), then sprinkle the onion on top. Bake covered for 1½ hours in an oven pre-heated to 375 degrees. During the final 15 minutes of baking time, stir in the mushrooms. Serves four.

Rabbit Pie

3 cups rabbit meat
½ stick butter
1 green pepper, chopped
1 medium onion, chopped
¼ cup flour
2 cups rabbit broth
salt
pepper

Parboil rabbit pieces until they are tender and will easily come away from the bone with a fork. Chop and shred the meat into small pieces until you have the required 3 cups. Melt the butter in a large skillet, then sauté the pepper and onion until tender (5 minutes). Blend in the flour until the mixture just begins to bubble. Gradually pour in the rabbit broth (made separately by boiling rabbit ribs and belly flesh, or you can use the liquid the meat was parboiled in), stirring constantly. Add just a pinch of salt and pepper to taste and continue cooking until the sauce in the pan is thick and smooth. Add the cooked rabbit meat to the sauce, heat thoroughly, then transfer to a large, shallow baking dish. Next, prepare the pie crust.

Pie Crust
1 cup flour
¼ cup vegetable shortening
½ teaspoon salt
2 tablespoons cold water

Blend the salt and flour together, then with a fork thoroughly mix in the shortening, occasionally sprinkling with just a tiny bit of the cold water to moisten. On a lightly floured surface, roll out the dough until it is the right size to fit the top of your shallow baking dish. Place the pie crust on top of the dish containing the rabbit and sauce, and with your fingers crimp it around the edges, then make several small slits in the top of the crust to allow steam to escape. Bake the rabbit pie in an oven pre-heated to 425 degrees for 15 minutes or until the dough is done and pie-crust brown. Serves four.

Farm-style Barbecued Rabbit
2 rabbits, cut into pieces
1 large jar Open Pit Barbecue Sauce

Arrange the pieces of rabbit in the bottom of a roasting pan, then pour the barbecue sauce over the top. Bake slowly in an oven pre-heated to 325 degrees for 2 to 2½ hours. After the first hour of cooking, turn the rabbit pieces in the pan, using a basting brush if necessary to ensure all pieces are well coated with the sauce. Serves four.

Broiled Rabbit
2 *young* rabbits, cut into pieces
½ cup butter, melted
2 teaspoons lemon juice

Arrange rabbit pieces on a broiling pan, baste with the butter and lemon juice which have been thoroughly mixed, then set the pan in your refrigerator to chill thoroughly for 1 hour. Then broil the rabbit in your oven, or over charcoal, for 30 to 45 minutes, turning and basting the pieces frequently. Serves four.

Baked Rabbit with Wild Rice
2 rabbits, cut into pieces
1 box Uncle Ben's Long Grain and Wild Rice
1 can condensed cream of mushroom soup

Parboil the meat and when it is tender remove it from the bones with a fork and shred into small pieces. Prepare the wild rice per instructions on the box. When the rice is cooked, thoroughly mix in the rabbit meat and mushroom soup. Transfer to a lightly buttered glass casserole dish, cover, and bake 1 hour in an oven pre-heated to 350 degrees. Serves four.

Rabbit Stew
1 large rabbit
2 medium onions, chopped
2 potatoes, cut into chunks
1 can beef bouillon
2 stalks celery, sliced
1 green pepper, chopped
1 cup mushrooms
4 carrots, sliced
1 teaspoon salt
¼ teaspoon black pepper
¼ teaspoon thyme
cold water

Parboil the rabbit pieces and when they are tender remove the meat from the bones and cut into bite-size chunks. Lightly dust these chunks of meat with flour and then brown in a skillet containing cooking oil. Then add all of the ingredients to a large pot and just enough cold water to cover. Simmer slowly on low heat for 2 hours, adding more water if the stew is too thick. Serves four.

Favorite Squirrel Recipes

Nearly all of the recipes just described for rabbit work equally well with red or gray squirrels. However, you'll have to keep in mind that squirrels are invariably smaller than rabbits, so accordingly adjust your required amount of meat for each recipe (the meat of three squirrels about equals that of two rabbits). Also, in the cases of broiling and panfrying squirrels, slightly less cooking time is required.

In addition to the previous recipes, following are still others, specifically intended for squirrels, that will please all comers.

Squirrel Slumgullion
2 squirrels, cut into pieces
1 quart cold water
½ teaspoon salt
¼ teaspoon black pepper
1 large can tomatoes (with liquid)
1 medium onion, chopped
2 carrots, chopped
1 green pepper, chopped
1 bay leaf, crumbled
½ teaspoon mixed herbs
rice or noodles

Parboil the squirrel pieces until the meat is tender, then remove the meat from the bones with a fork and shred it into bite-size pieces. Add the squirrel meat to a large pot, add all the remaining ingredients (except the rice or noodles) and bring to a boil. Then, reduce the heat, cover the pot, and simmer slowly for ½ hour. Meanwhile, prepare 2 cups uncooked rice or noodles per instructions on the package. Thoroughly mix the rice or noodles with the squirrel slumgullion and serve on a hot platter. (Remember to pour off the water before adding the rice or noodles to the squirrel). Serves four.

Deepfried Squirrel
2 squirrels, cut into pieces
6 egg yolks
½ cup cracker crumbs
vegetable oil
salt
pepper

Parboil the squirrel pieces for 15 minutes until they are almost tender. Then remove from the water and pat dry with paper towels. Mix just a pinch of salt and pepper in a bowl, then beat in the egg yolks. Dip each squirrel in the mix, then roll in the cracker crumbs until completely coated. Gently drop the squirrel pieces one at a time into a pot of hot cooking oil (or use a deepfrying basket) for 6 to 8 minutes or until golden brown. Serves four.

Country Squirrel Delight
2 or 3 squirrels, cut into pieces
flour
vegetable oil
water
1 large onion, sliced
salt
pepper

Rub just a bit of salt and pepper into the squirrel pieces, then thoroughly brown the meat in a skillet containing ¼ inch of cooking oil. Remove the squirrels from the pan and set aside. Drain the cooking oil from the pan and stir about ¼ cup of flour into the pan drippings. Continually stir on low heat until the flour-paste just begins to brown, then add just a bit of water and continue to stir to form a rich gravy. Stir in the onion, just a pinch more salt and pepper, then place the squirrel back in the pan. Cover the skillet and simmer on very low heat for 2 hours, occasionally adding just a bit more water if necessary. Serves four.

Brunswick Stew

2 squirrels, cut into pieces
1 large onion, sliced
1 quart tomatoes (with liquid)
⅛ teaspoon red cayenne pepper
¼ teaspoon thyme
3 potatoes, diced
1 cup lima beans
1 cup corn
1 teaspoon sugar
1 teaspoon salt
½ teaspoon black pepper
bacon fat

Parboil the squirrel pieces in lightly salted water until they are almost tender. Carefully remove the meat from the bones in large chunks. Dredge the chunks of squirrel meat with flour and then brown them lightly, along with the onions, in a skillet containing several tablespoons of bacon fat. Add water to cover the meat and then add the potatoes, tomatoes, cayenne pepper, thyme, sugar, salt and pepper. Cover the pan and cook on low heat for ½ hour. Then add the lima beans and corn and continue simmering until the vegetables are done and tender. Just before serving, you can thin the stew a bit if you wish with a little hot water. Or, if you like, you can stir in just a bit of flour, cornstarch or breadcrumbs to make it thicker. Serves four.

Hearty Squirrel Casserole

2 squirrels, cut into pieces
1 large onion, diced
3 potatoes, cut into chunks
1 medium can tomatoes (with liquid)
flour
salt
pepper

Rub just a bit of salt and pepper into each piece of squirrel, then dredge with flour and brown on all sides in a skillet containing bacon fat or cooking oil. Next, in a deep glass casserole dish layer pieces of squirrel, onion and potatoes. Pour the tomatoes and liquid over the top, cover the dish, and bake in an oven pre-heated to 350 degrees for 1½ hours. Serves four.

Ozark Squirrel with Mushrooms
2 or 3 squirrels, cut into pieces
6 strips bacon
flour
½ teaspoon garlic powder
¼ teaspoon thyme
¼ cup tomato paste
½ cup red wine
1 can chicken stock
1 cup mushrooms

Fry the bacon until it is done, then set aside on a paper towel to drain. Crumble the bacon pieces. Next, flour the squirrel pieces and brown on all sides in the bacon fat in the pan. Stir in the garlic powder, thyme and tomato sauce. Pour the wine and chicken stock over the squirrel, cover the pan, and cook on low heat for 1 hour. Fifteen minutes before the end of the required cooking time, thoroughly mix in the bacon bits and mushrooms. Serves four.

'Possum, 'Coon and Other Small-Game Recipes

Ask any old-timer who lives far back in some remote hill-country hide-away what his favorite meal is and instead of some well-known food such as steak, chicken or pork chops, he's as likely to say, with a twinkle in his eye, "'Possum and sweet 'taters." Ask another and you'll just as likely hear "roast 'coon," or "muskrat ragout," or perhaps some recipe involving groundhog or beaver. Each of these creatures falls into the category of small game and all can be delicious if and when-ever a sportsman happens to take one with a firearm. In those cases in which a particular species cannot be legally hunted, such as 'possum, muskrat or beaver, make friends with a local trapper and there's a good chance he'll give you all the meat you want after he's carefully removed the pelts. After questioning a number of friends who partake of this unconventional dining, and talking with old-timers, I've found that the following recipes shake out on top as the most popular.

Some might disagree, but woodchuck, 'possum and coon are delicious. In remote country areas, they've been staple dinner meats for generations.

Roast Beaver
1 whole, rough-dressed beaver
1 large onion, sliced
salt
pepper

Carefully remove as much fat as possible from the beaver carcass, then rub a bit of salt and pepper into the skin and inside the body cavity. Place the beaver in a deep roasting pan, then place the pan in an oven pre-heated to 475 degrees for 15 minutes to sear the outside of the carcass. Next, drape the onion slices over the top of the beaver, then reduce the heat to 325 degrees and roast, uncovered, for 30 minutes per pound. Every 20 minutes or so, gently tilt the roasting pan and spoon away the grease drippings that have accumulated in the bottom of the pan.

'Possum and Sweet 'Taters
1 whole, rough-dressed opossum
2 teaspoons salt
½ teaspoon black pepper
¾ cup water
¼ cup flour
4 medium sweet potatoes (or yams)
2 tablespoons brown sugar

The opossum should be skinned with feet, tail and head removed. Be sure any fat is trimmed away from the carcass. Wash thoroughly with warm water, then drain and rub inside the body cavity and outside with salt and pepper. Next, rub flour into the skin with your fingers, both inside and outside. Lay the opossum on its back in a deep roasting pan as you would a turkey, add ½ cup hot water to the bottom of the pan, cover the pan with a lid and bake in an oven pre-heated to 350 degrees for 1 hour. Meanwhile, peel the sweet potatoes or yams and split them lengthwise into halves, then again into quarters if you like. Arrange the potatoes around the opossum in the bottom of the pan, add the remaining ¼ cup of water, cover and bake 30 minutes longer. Remove the cover from the pan and sprinkle the potatoes with the brown sugar and just a bit of salt. Now turn the oven up to 400 degrees and continue baking a short while longer until the opossum is brown and the potatoes have a glazed appearance. Serves four.

Stuffed 'Coon
1 whole, rough-dressed raccoon
vinegar
cold water
1 apple, peeled and sliced
1 package prepared stuffing mix

The raccoon should be skinned, with the head, feet and tail removed. Remove any fat deposits you see and with the tip of your knife blade cut out the scent glands or "kernels" found under the front legs and rear legs. Place the 'coon in a large pot, add 1 tablespoon vinegar, then fill the pot with cold water until the 'coon is entirely covered. Bring the water to a boil, let the cauldron bubble a full 5 minutes, then discard the water. Start again with fresh cold water and another tablespoon of vinegar, bring to a boil and simmer another 5 minutes. Repeat this procedure as many times as necessary until no foamy scum appears on the surface of the water (generally, three "washes" are necessary with young 'coons, four with older animals). When the water continues to boil clear, remove the 'coon, drain, pat dry with paper toweling, then set in your refrigerator for ½ hour or until the carcass is entirely cooled. Meanwhile, prepare your stuffing. A highly seasoned bread stuffing is recommended. Place the 'coon in a deep roasting pan and add the apple slices to the body cavity. Then add the stuffing, being careful not to pack it too tightly to allow for expansion. Baste the outside of the 'coon with melted butter, place a lid on the roasting pan, then bake in an oven pre-heated to 300 degrees for 4 hours. One-half hour before the end of the required baking time, remove the lid from the pan, baste the 'coon again with butter and sprinkle lightly with flour to produce a burnished, crispy appearance. Repeat this twice at 10-minute intervals. Serves four.

Muskrat 'n Brown Gravy
2 muskrats, cut into pieces
vinegar
flour
salt
pepper
vegetable oil
1 can sweet condensed milk

Place the muskrat pieces in a deep bowl, add 1 tablespoon vinegar and then cover with 1 quart of cold water. Cover the bowl and place in your refrigerator overnight. The following day, rinse the muskrat pieces in fresh water and pat dry with paper toweling. Mix just a bit of salt and pepper into a little flour, dust the muskrat pieces, then brown on all sides in a skillet containing hot cooking oil. Cover the pan, reduce the heat, and continue to cook slowly for 1 hour (add just a bit more oil if necessary). When the meat is tender, remove it from the pan to some place where it will stay warm. Drain off nearly all the cooking oil from the skillet. To the several tablespoons of drippings and grease remaining in the pan, add 3 or 4 tablespoons of flour, stirring continually. Then stir in the canned milk and continue to stir until it is very hot, but do not allow it to come to a boil. When the gravy thickens to your liking, pour it over the muskrat and serve. Serves four.

Woodchuck Burgers
1 woodchuck, cut into pieces
½ cup bread crumbs
⅛ cup onion, diced
2 eggs, beaten
salt
pepper

Parboil the woodchuck pieces until the meat is almost tender, then remove the meat from the bones with a fork. Next, run the meat through your grinder (only once, through the coarse blade). Add a little of the bread crumbs, the onion, and just a pinch of salt and pepper. Knead well with your hands. Then form into hamburger-size patties, dunk each in the beaten egg, then roll thoroughly in the remaining bread crumbs. Fry until golden brown. Serves four.

13

Freezing
Fish and Game

Whenever a greater quantity of fish or game is brought home than a sportsman's family can consume in one or two meals, freezing the remainder for future use is the easiest, quickest and most effective method of preservation.

Many people, this scribe included, even look upon the cold storage of large quantities of fish and game as a real "turn on." Maybe this is due to the latent packrat tendencies most of us harbor, or the "be prepared" scouting philosophies we were subjected to as youngsters. Whatever the explanation, we're living in terribly uncertain — even scary — economic times, and there's an undeniably warm, smug sense of security in knowing the freezer is chock-full of venison roasts, burger, quail, ducks, rabbits and a variety of fish. If you've got a vegetable garden as well, to supplement your fish and game dinners, you've got a sound hedge against inflation and also a real lifesaver, both literally and figuratively, should there ever occur some type of unforeseen emergency.

But all of this depends upon whether the hunter or fisherman has given the matter some advance thought. If not, he's in for a sad and displeasing reunion with his quarry the next time he plucks some item or another from the deep freezer.

It should be emphasized that freezing fish and game is only an intermediate step between the field (or water) and the table. So the reader may wish to refer back to earlier chapters having to do with dressing or butchering fish or game, interim storage methods and transportation techniques. After all, freezing is no cure-all, and the final taste test is largely influenced by the quality and condition of the meat before it was submitted to its long-term cold storage.

Preparing Fish and Game for Storage

If an outdoorsman remembers nothing else, he should memorize the five basic steps to freezing fish and game successfully:
 – Clean the meat
 – Wrap it airtight
 – Freeze small packages
 – Freeze it fast
 – Freeze it at low temperatures
Properly cleaning the meat prior to freezing is of paramount concern because unwanted, damaged or bloodied tissue can adversely affect the meat's flavor.

In the case of fish, never freeze any species with its entrails still in the body; ditto for removing the gills in the case of those fish to be frozen whole. Take steaks, fillets or whole, rough-dressed fish and hold them under a light stream of cold running water and with your fingertips rub away any traces of blood or slime.

As a general rule, if fish are to be frozen for less than two months, no additional pre-freezing treatment is necessary beyond filleting or dressing the fish in the desired manner and then cleaning them as described above. But if fish are to remain in cold storage for longer than two months, just prior to freezing they should be dipped in some type of soaking solution to delay rancidity and the effects of oxidation. Lean or white-fleshed fish (bass, walleyes, panfish, etc.) should be dunked in a cold brine solution for about two minutes; make the brine by dissolving one cup of salt in a gallon of water (or, instead of using salt, squirt a healthy shot of lemon juice into the water and stir well). Fatty, oily or red-fleshed fish (salmon, trout, etc.) should be dipped in an ascorbic acid solution (ascorbic acid is available in some grocery stores or from your pharmacist) and the dip is easily made by dissolving 16 teaspoons of the compound in a gallon of water. Again, soak the fish about two minutes, then shake off any excess liquid before proceeding with further wrapping operations.

Upland gamebirds and waterfowl should be carefully trimmed of fatty deposits lying near the surface of the skin and any other remnants of loose tissue. Take the time to pick out and remove any shot pellets that are visible. If there is only minor bloodshot damage, soak the meat in salt water, but severe bloodshot areas should be trimmed away cleanly. Make sure all feathers, scales (from the legs) and other unwanted matter are removed so they do not remain in direct contact with the meat for prolonged periods of time while in cold storage. Finally, rinse the birds in cold water, but only for the minimal time necessary to flush away dirt or other debris.

Light-colored red meats, typically from small-game animals such as rabbits, can be washed with cold water to remove dirt and other unwanted matter. Again, trim away fat deposits, loose skin remnants, and severely damaged pieces of meat, and pluck out any visible pellets. In the case of minor bloodshot areas, there is no alternative but to soak the meat in water, but make sure you've added one cup of salt per gallon.

Dark-colored red meats (venison, bear, etc.) should never be washed with water or allowed to soak, with one exception: you can and should soak the heart and liver in a salt-water bath for 24 hours to draw out blood that will have clotted inside these organs. Prepare a solution of one cup of salt per gallon of water, and after the first eight hours of soaking time discard the bloody water and prepare a fresh solution.

The remainder of the meat should be trimmed of all fat or tallow, loose skin remnants and shot-damaged tissue. Also trim away all bloodshot areas. Use a soft bristle brush to wipe away surface debris

Cling-wraps such as foil, cellophane or Saran prevent "travel" by locking in moisture and locking out dry-cold freezer air.

such as dirt, then lightly dab the skin with a paper towel moistened with a bit of vinegar or cold water to which you've added a bit of baking soda.

Once the fish or game in question has been cleaned and otherwise readied for freezing, consider wrapping materials and procedures. Of great importance is the subject of "travel," but we're not referring here to away-from-home trips that take hunters and fishermen to new places and exciting adventures.

The kind of travel all sportsmen should strive to eliminate involves a reciprocal transfer of moisture in which cold, dry freezer air sometimes works its way into wrapped packages to draw out and displace the moisture contained in the flesh of frozen meats. The end result can be discoloration, freezer burn in which the meat becomes dried out and rancid, or crystallization in which frost particles permeate the meat fibers and cause it to be blah and mushy tasting when it is later defrosted and then cooked by the method of your choice.

There are several ways to eliminate this kind of travel and the easiest involves nothing more than instituting a moisture or vapor barrier in the form of certain wrapping materials. This keeps the dry, cold freezer air out, and the meat's moisture in.

Cling wraps have a high resistance to moisture-vapor transmission and therefore are the best bet. Clear plastic, heavy-duty cellophane, Saran wrap and aluminum foil are good choices as all can be pressed tightly against and around all surfaces of irregularly shaped meats to eliminate air pockets and at the same time prevent dry freezer air from seeping in.

Some sportsmen may be tempted to buy one variation or another of the so-called freezer bags now available in most grocery stores. It's my opinion—nothing more—that these are better suited to freezing bulk quantities of vegetables than meats, because it is very difficult to eliminate air pockets. What you have to do, after inserting the meat, is to seal almost the entire length of the Ziploc closure except for one corner, squeeze out as much air as possible by hand, then place your mouth over the open corner and suck the remaining air from the bag. In this manner, you'll create a vacuum inside the bag, causing it to collapse and in so doing tightly hug the irregular surfaces of the meat inside. This can require a bit of manual dexterity, because once the air has been sucked out of the bag, you briefly have to maintain the sucking operation as you quickly pinch the corner of the bag

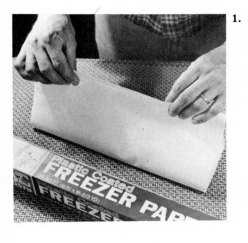

1. The popular drugstore fold conserves paper and provides the tightest wrap. To make it, first raise the edges of the paper between two fingers.

2. Then fold the paper down until it is flat on top of the package.

3. Next fold over the corners.

4. Finally, tuck the corners under and seal the package edges with masking tape. Be sure to label the package properly so you know what's inside and the date it was frozen.

shut and then continue sealing the remainder of the closure device.

After your fish or game has been enclosed in this first wrap, be it a cling wrap or plastic freezer bag, it's wise to wrap it a second time in white, plastic-coated freezer wrapping paper for added protection. Use the popular drugstore fold to conserve paper (which is quite expensive) and also for the tightest wrap. This unique fold is accomplished by first laying out a rectangular sheet of paper and placing the fish or game squarely in the middle. Bring up the top and bottom edges of the paper and, holding them together in the middle of the meat, fold them as many times as necessary (usually three or four) to bring them down snug and flat against the top of the meat. Then take the tail of the paper extending at one end and fold it inward on both sides to create a triangular flap which can then be tucked under at that side. Finally, repeat this procedure at the other end.

When the second wrap is completed, use masking tape to seal the various paper ends and edges; common cellophane tape is worthless in this task as it will come loose shortly after being subjected to the freezer's cold temperatures. The last step is to use a felt-tipped pen containing indelible ink to label the outside of each package as to the kind of meat inside, its weight or size, and the date it was frozen.

Freezer Tricks That Work

By far, the best way to freeze small game, upland birds, waterfowl or big-game meat is by double-wrapping them as just described. The method also is ideal for fish, but there are two other fish-freezing methods that work just as well, if not better.

If adequate freezer space is available, authorities recommend freezing your fish in water. You'll need a number of empty half-gallon or gallon paper milk cartons that have been thoroughly washed out. Simply place in each container the number of fish fillets, steaks or whole, rough-dressed fish your family requires for a meal. Then fill each milk carton with cold water until all of the fish are amply covered. The secret behind the success of this method is that the fish is frozen inside a solid block of ice and this prevents any loss of moisture from the flesh or any introduction of dry freezer air. However, I should

The best way to freeze small fish is in water in milk cartons. With the fish in a solid block of ice, freezer air cannot seep in to cause deterioration.

mention two words of advice. Leave an inch or so of space at the top of the milk carton, to allow for the expansion of the water as it freezes. Also, don't crowd too many fish inside a single milk carton as this will prevent each from being encased in its own cocoon of solid ice. So, when freezing a large quantity of fish, use as many milk cartons as necessary. When each milk carton is filled with fish and water, I close the top back to its original folded shape and then staple it firmly closed. Then, as usual, mark the outside with a felt-tipped pen so you know the nature of the contents.

A slight variation of this method is freezing fish in heavy-duty Ziploc poly bags, which come in a wide variety of sizes. All you have to do is place the fish in the bag, fill the bag to within two inches of the top with water, seal, and place in your freezer.

If freezer space is limited, yet you've found your fish are more flavorful and fresh tasting by freezing in water, another freezing trick is glazing. First wrap your fish as tightly as possible in plastic-coated freezer wrapping paper, skipping the first cling-wrap step. Place this fish in your freezer and at the same time place in the freezer a clean, gallon paper milk carton filled two-thirds full with cold water. In several hours the fish should be frozen solid, and the water in the milk carton should be icy cold, almost ready to freeze itself. Remove the carton from the freezer and set it on your table. Now remove the fish packages and very carefully unwrap them. Then, dip each fish, fillet or steak in the icy cold water and quickly remove it. Hold it aloft for several seconds, then dip again. Then dip a third time. This procedure will see the formation of a glaze or repeated thin layers of ice form on the outside of the fish, which can then be wrapped up again in the same freezer wrapping paper. What you've achieved is the same block method of freezing fish in ice but without the space-consuming milk cartons.

Most frozen fish will remain in good condition for six months but after that begin gradually to show signs of rancidity. Some fish species with a high oil content, however, such as steelhead trout and salmon, should be used within three months, before enzymatic changes begin to reduce flavor and change the texture of the meat.

Most fowl, big-game and small-game species also will remain in good condition for many months but after a certain period likewise begin to reveal rancidity. Upland birds, for example, can be frozen for up to a year, but use them within six to nine months if possible.

Red meats such as venison can be stored in your freezer for up to a year, but it is best to make use of thick cuts such as roasts within nine months and thin cuts such as round steaks and tenderloins within six months. Waterfowl species, most of which have a high oil content in their flesh, should not be frozen for periods in excess of six months. Small game can be frozen whole, in quarters or in disjointed pieces and will remain in good condition for up to one year.

It's best to flash-freeze fish and game meats. Turn your temperature dial as low as it will go prior to placing packages of meat inside. Add packages only a few at a time, then more later. Some refrigerator-freezer combinations are incapable of flash-freezing. Best are chest-type freezers with lift-up lids.

But let's backtrack for just a moment to discuss one other crucially important aspect of freezing fish and game. Whatever the species, fish and game should always be quick-frozen or flash-frozen and then maintained at a freezer temperature of somewhere between 0 degrees to 16 degrees Fahrenheit. This is a key step in preserving freshness and flavor, because a slower freezing time at a higher temperature will allow ice crystals to form on the flesh.

To accomplish quick-freezing, turn the temperature dial of your freezer compartment down to its coldest setting about two hours ahead of time. Then place the individual packages of fish or game as close to the insides of the freezer walls as possible as this is where the coils or elements are located. Also, ensure that none of the packages are allowed to contact each other.

The following day, when all of the packages are frozen solid, you can return the freezer's temperature dial to its original setting (no higher than 16 degrees Fahrenheit) and stack or arrange the packages any way you desire.

If your freezer is a smaller one, don't overload it with packages to be quick-frozen as you'll be working against yourself; the sudden introduction of a large quantity of warm meat drastically reduces the freezer's cooling capacity. The best bet is to place all of your wrapped meat packages in your refrigerator overnight. The following day, pre-condition your freezer by turning down the temperature dial as described, then add only half of the well-chilled packages from your refrigerator. The next day, add the other half (or appropriate lesser quantities every several hours). Of course, when freezing fish in water, begin with ice-cold water and the flash-freezing time will be far less than if the water was only cool to begin with.

In some instances, quick-freezing is not possible with certain types of freezer-refrigerator combinations. Some of the newer, energy efficient models and also those which have self-defrosting capabilities can rarely achieve temperatures below 20 degrees. Although foods can be frozen solidly at this temperature, they should be used within one month because any bacterial action may not be entirely curtailed to preserve the meat for longer periods. One alternative, especially if you freeze large quantities of meat such as an occasional elk, plus have a vegetable garden and other freezing needs, is to consider buying an upright or chest-type freezer.

I personally prefer a chest-type freezer to an upright because studies have shown lowboys with lift-up lids are more efficient than stand-up models with swing-out doors. It's simply a matter of physics and the basic principle of cold air always sinking to its lowest possible level. When you open the door of an upright freezer, the cold air formerly trapped inside quickly sinks and rushes out the bottom and is replaced by warm air from the room coming in at the top. Hence, when you close the door, the electricity must immediately kick on and the freezer must work hard for half an hour or longer to return the inner temperature to what it was before you opened the door. With a chest-type freezer, you open the top lid and the bulk of cold air remains trapped inside as there is no opening down low allowing it to escape. A bit of warm air will indeed come in the top, but not nearly as much as with a stand-up freezer, and when the lid is quickly closed again the freezer will have to turn on only momentarily to return its confines to the former temperature.

If you can't afford a chest or upright freezer just now, and your freezer-refrigerator combination is incapable of flash-freezing fish and game, one choice is to take your wrapped packages of fish and game to your local butcher. If you are a regular customer he will probably be glad to flash-freeze your meat, for free or at nominal charge, in one of his ultra-cold storage lockers. The next day, you can transfer the packages to your home freezer.

Or maybe you can use a neighbor's freezer overnight, plying him in advance of course with a couple of nice trout, a venison roast or a pheasant for his own family.

How to Defrost Fish and Game

Defrosting fish or game for a meal should never be rushed because subjecting meat to a rapid temperature change causes unnecessary softness in the texture of the meat, in extreme cases even giving it a "wilted" appearance. So be patient, and go slowly.

There are two absolutely horrible ways to defrost any kind of fish or game meat, and since they are so prevalent today I should describe them and strongly discourage their use. One of the most common sins simply involves poor planning. Somebody wants fish for dinner, so a package is grabbed from the freezer and held under a stream of warm tap water to defrost it. Thanks for the dinner invitation, but I think I'll grab a greasy burger downtown.

The other *faux pas* is removing a package of fish or game from the freezer and letting it just sit and defrost on a drainboard for several hours. What happens is that the outer portions of the meat defrost first and then sit there at room temperature waiting for the inner portions to defrost. Housewives manage to get away with this abhorrent practice because the beef, pork and other domestic meats they commonly defrost are pumped full of sundry additives and chemical preservatives. Fish and game are not, and every minute in which they are subjected to room temperatures spells just that much more deterioration in flavor and freshness.

There is one exception to this rule and it has to do with fish frozen in water in plastic bags or paper milk cartons. In this case there is not much harm in speeding up the thawing of the ice by holding the bag or milk carton under a stream of very cold water until the outside ice covering is largely melted away and the fish inside just barely beginning to appear.

However, to play it entirely safe, the best possible method for defrosting fish and game is to remove the package from your freezer and place it overnight in your refrigerator. This way, the meat defrosts but still remains very cold as it is doing so. While this sounds simple enough, there is one cardinal error that is committed too often, and that is allowing either the fish or game meat to soak in icy melt water or its own juices. When this happens, the water or juice quickly becomes stale, even if cold, and is reabsorbed by the meat which may later reveal an unpleasant taste.

If your fish are frozen in water in a milk carton, use a knife to remove the carton so all you have is a block of ice with the fish inside. If your fish are frozen in water in a plastic bag, cut the plastic and peel it away. Set the ice-encased fish in a colander, with the top covered with a damp towel, and set the colander on its legs in a deep pan, or supported by its rim in a deep bowl or pot. This prevents the accumulation of icy melt water, allowing it to gradually drain away as the ice melts. Yet, as the fish are slowly revealed, the damp towel continues to keep them moist.

Basically the same approach should be taken when defrosting fish frozen in cling wraps and wrapping paper as well as upland gamebirds, waterfowl, small game and big game. Don't let them soak in their own juices as they defrost. Unwrap the meat, place it in a colander in a deep pan in your refrigerator, cover with a damp cloth, and let the juices slowly drain away and collect in the vessel underneath so they may later be discarded.

Last, no type of meat that has been frozen and then defrosted should ever be re-frozen again in its present state. Ideally, the meat should be cooked and eaten within 36 hours of being defrosted. However, once you've cooked a particular meal and have leftovers, they indeed can be safely frozen because the entire personality of the meat has undergone such a radical change that it is like starting all over

A good rule when defrosting fish or game is not to let the meat defrost at room temperature. Above all, don't let the meat soak in melt water and juices. Unwrap the frozen package and set the meat in a colander in your refrigerator overnight. Cover with a damp towel. As the meat defrosts, it will remain cold, yet the juices and melt water will drain away into the pan underneath.

with fresh food. So if you defrost fish, rabbit, venison—anything—for a meal and as you are cooking discover you have far more than you really need, never return it to your freezer. Go ahead and cook it anyway, then freeze the cooked dish later.

In freezing cooked fish and game meats, I like to use heavy plastic freezer bags with Ziploc closures; you can even freeze soups and stews in these. Or, in any housewares department you'll find a wide variety of sizes and shapes of plastic freezer boxes with snap-top lids. In a pinch, I've even been known to set an entire glass casserole dish in the freezer. It works fine, if you're willing temporarily to forgo the use of that cookware for other needs.

When defrosting such pre-cooked foods, follow the same strategy as with uncooked foods; that is, take it slow and easy by allowing them to defrost overnight in your refrigerator.

Index